SHAPING THE PRAYERS OF THE PEOPLE

SHAPING
THE PRAYERS
OF THE PEOPLE

The Art of Intercession

Samuel Wells and Abigail Kocher

WILLIAM B. EERDMANS PUBLISHING COMPANY
Grand Rapids, Michigan / Cambridge, U.K.

First published in 2013 by Canterbury Press, Norwich,
as *Crafting Prayers for Public Worship: The Art of Intercession* by Samuel Wells

This edition published 2014 by
WM. B. EERDMANS PUBLISHING CO.
2140 Oak Industrial Drive N.E., Grand Rapids, Michigan 49505 /
P.O. Box 163, Cambridge CB3 9PU U.K.

Printed in the United States of America

20 19 18 17 16 15   7 6 5 4 3 2

Library of Congress Cataloging-in-Publication Data

Wells, Samuel, 1965-
Shaping the prayers of the people : the art of intercession /
Samuel Wells and Abigail Kocher.
pages   cm
Includes bibliographical references
ISBN 978-0-8028-7097-1 (pbk. : alk. paper)
1. Intercessory prayer — Christianity.   I. Title.

BV210.3.W45   2014
248.3´2 — dc23

2014015097

www.eerdmans.com

For Caroline Kocher

CONTENTS

PREFACE

THIS BOOK ENDEAVORS TO MAKE intercessory prayer, in its recognition of our particular human need, our common dependence on God, and our growing expectation that God will bless us, a formative practice for the church.

It arose when Sam Wells invited me to adapt his work on prayer, written in a British context, so that it might speak more fully to an American audience. I wondered initially whether the differences between the two cultures of worship might overshadow the similarities. In England there is a pervasive liturgical tradition — that of the Church of England, for centuries enshrined in the 1662 *Book of Common Prayer,* and, more lately, in the materials published since 2000 known as *Common Worship* — with a variety of Protestant, largely non-liturgical, traditions on one side and Roman Catholicism on the other. Sam lived and pastored in the United States for several years. He discovered how challenging it is, by comparison, to generalize about churches here — within each respective denomination as much as for the "mainline" as a whole. There is no single pervasive tradition. Yet I perceived, and he agreed, that there is nonetheless something significant to be said about congregational intercessory prayer that transcends denominational differences, styles of worship, and physical settings. So I took up the challenge, and this is what emerged. If you pick up a copy of the British sister volume *Crafting Prayers for Public Worship: The Art of Intercession* (Norwich: Canterbury, 2013), you will see the two volumes have some significant differences; and you will notice there is an additional chapter in this American edition.

A great company of God's people have been insisting for some time that a book like this be written — among them many who have worshiped at Duke Chapel or heard prayers offered at settings more broadly in Durham, North Carolina, and beyond. Instinct and conviction suggests that intercessory prayer is lived in the moment, and that the best way to teach is by inspiration and example rather than the written word: so a good deal of resistance, particularly in Sam, had to be broken down before this volume seemed timely. The way of praying described here was shaped in the context of Duke Chapel, a large, ecumenical community gathered around an extraordinary place of worship. The Chapel serves Duke University but also has a ministry to a much wider community through its renowned music, preaching, and worship and increasingly through its social outreach and interfaith programs. During his time as Dean of the Chapel, Sam began to find that though he was primarily there to preach, people particularly commented on the prayers. And though the preaching was mostly his, leading the prayers was a role he shared with a number of colleagues. Thus he was challenged to articulate for himself and describe to others his convictions about intercessory prayer and what it might mean to do it well. The publication of this book is due, in great part, to the repeated requests and encouragements, not to say nagging, of many, among them Emily Wilson-Hauger, Stanley Hauerwas, Sally Robinson, Norman Wirzba, Rebekah Eklund, Charles Michael Smith, Jackie Strange, and Adrienne Koch. Emily Wilson-Hauger in particular secretly filed away copies of a good number of prayers that would otherwise have been casually discarded; and Rebekah Eklund generously sorted and ordered them into categories and strands. Craig Kocher and Jo Bailey Wells have been faithful companions, trusted scrutinizers, kind evaluators, and partners in ministry at every stage.

The congregation, clergy, and community of Duke Chapel incubated much of what is described in these pages. The insights distilled in this book were explored alongside Craig Kocher, Meghan Feldmeyer, Nancy Ferree-Clark, Keith Daniel, Adam Hollowell, Gaston Warner, Christy Lohr Sapp, Kori Jones, Bruce Puckett, and other pastoral and musical colleagues. Such companions in prayer enriched and deepened the imagination about how prayer could be shared in a spirit of ecumenical generosity among mainline Protestants. Several of the example prayers that appear in this book were offered first at Duke Chapel.

In discerning the distinctively American flavor of this volume I am especially grateful to the following people, both clergy and laity, who shared at some length with me insights, resonances, and tensions with their own Lutheran, United Methodist, Presbyterian, and Episcopalian practices of congregational prayer: Andie Wigodsky Rohrs, Margie Nea, Phillip Martin, Robin Steinke, Mark Oldenburg, Griff Gatewood, Alex Evans, Scott Chrostek, Wendy Chrostek, and Michelle Shrader. In particular Ed Phillips shaped my appreciation and understanding significantly through offering an illuminating historical perspective on how distinct types of congregational prayer developed in the American context.

Practices of leading prayer are shaped in the midst of congregations.

With sincere gratitude I give thanks for the season praying with Reveille United Methodist Church in Richmond, Virginia, where I most recently served. Sam now enjoys the privilege of sharing in prayer with the people of St. Martin-in-the-Fields in London, England, where he is vicar. A number of the example prayers published here arose in these two settings.

For Sam, this book begins with the prayers of his parents kneeling at his bedside, and with the congregational prayers of St. Mary's Church, Salt-ford, Bristol, England, where he grew up. For me, this book begins in the congregation in whose company I first came to know prayer: First United Methodist Church in Rocky Mount, North Carolina. And it continues with my parents, who first lived daily patterns of prayer with me and taught me what to hope for and how to ask. And in that spirit it is dedicated to my daughter, with whom prayer is a cherished practice, renewed every day. My intercessory prayer is that she will become a blessing to others beyond even what she has been to me: which would truly be an awesome work of God.

ABIGAIL KOCHER

INTRODUCTION

"IT IS OUR DUTY AND OUR JOY." These words, familiar in the Lutheran prayer of thanksgiving in the service of Holy Communion, are equally fitting for the practice of intercession.[1] Interceding in public worship is a duty; this book is intended to make it a joy.

It is a joy when it is an opportunity to engage in passionate and whole-hearted dialogue with the maker, redeemer, and sustainer of all things: when one is invited to commune in the heart of God and share one's deepest fears, hopes, and realities. It is a joy when one can meet the intersection between the profoundest longings of one's soul, the most direct import of the scripture, and the most desperate needs of the world. It is a joy when one can share this most intimate of encounters with a congregation one has joined for a season, for a morning, or for life. It is a joy when all one's disparate intimations of immortality, half-remembered wisdom, enchanting turns of phrase, abiding sense of outrage, restless pangs of despair, and reassuring rhythms of comfort can be brought together into one brief, tender, but comprehensive address to God.

But of course it's not always a joy. It's sometimes a tedious trudge through a lifeless hallway of half-hearted and tired phrases, delivered without passion by a leader going through the liturgical motions who never really reaches the people's hearts. Or occasionally it's an exercise in patience as an intercessor inflicts a social and political manifesto on a defenseless congregation in the presence of God. Some communities settle for the former because they are wary of the latter. It's possible to aspire beyond either. This book sets out to say why and show how.

---

1. These words are especially familiar to the Evangelical Lutheran Church in America. For their use in Holy Communion, see *Evangelical Lutheran Worship* (Minneapolis: Augsburg Fortress, 2006), p. 108.

PRAYING IN AMERICA

Though the inspiration for praying in the form of a collect is lodged in Anglican tradition, this book has a view to the more general context of American mainline denominations. Conversations with both laity and clergy representing Episcopalian, Lutheran (ELCA), United Methodist, and Presbyterian (PC[USA]) traditions shaped the scope of what is presented here. These denominations' styles of intercessory prayer are sufficiently similar to make their resonances rewarding, and are sufficiently distinct to make their differences illuminating.

In American mainline churches intercessions happen in broadly one of four ways. They may be read from a seasonally-produced denominational resource; selected from an official prayer book; written ahead of time by the pastor; or offered extemporaneously by the intercessor. The first two are more standardized; the last two present the opportunity for creativity and variety. Though the words are generated in a wide range of ways, it is likely that the intercessor (often without being aware) is drawing upon one of two historical threads well known in American Protestant experience. This is not merely a question of style but of the placement and expectation of intercessions in the liturgy.

What is sometimes known as the Pastoral Prayer is woven together from threads of the revivalist tradition. A pastoral prayer is comprehensive in the way that it often moves through other modes of prayer, such as confession and thanksgiving, before coming to intercessions. Led by the pastor, it seeks a heartfelt personal response and often has an emotive style. In some settings a musical underscore may be present and, when so, enhances these characteristic elements. This form of prayer has a history prior to reaching American shores, though. The Pastoral Prayer first took shape as part of the Reformation impulse to develop a form of prayer that addressed a specific time and place, named particular needs in the local community, and lifted up pastoral cares of the congregation. In many ways, the emergence of this form of prayer represented a desire among reformers not to return to prayers that had been previously printed. It offered the opportunity for clergy to articulate and author prayers on behalf of their congregations. Such prayer became a standard practice among Puritans and harkens back to the Reformed spirit Calvin sought to bring into practice in the church.

The other historical thread that shapes intercessions is most apparent in liturgy structured around Holy Communion, sometimes called word and table. Following this style, the intercessions take their own space separate from other forms of prayer, and they are often called Prayers of the People or Prayers of Intercession. In this format, prayers of confession, thanksgiving, and so forth have their own role in liturgy designed around the Eucharist. Joining in intercessions is understood to mean joining with the body of Christ, the church, in its ongoing worship of God throughout time and space; and weekly intercessions in corporate worship are seen to be part of the priestly work of the church.

These historical threads highlight the qualities that distinguish the present-day types of intercessory prayer encountered across mainline denominations. Congregations generally tend towards one more than the other, and the differences communicate a great deal about the beliefs and expectations a denomination or congregation has about intercessions.

PRAYING IN THE MAINLINE

One of the things that makes prayer in the American mainline ripe for imagination is the wide range of settings and styles of worship, not only between denominations, but within each denomination itself. This volume seeks to accept such a range of difference as an opportunity to inquire what prayer is really about and what people who pray, especially people who lead prayers, think they are doing.

One of the most obvious differences is that there are strong commitments about who leads the prayers in worship: whether it is a layperson or clergyperson, whether that person is the same or varies week to week. A variety of factors are at work here, including denominational standards, size of the congregation, number of clergy available, and expectation for lay involvement in worship. What is illuminating to see is that commitments about who leads prayer are not simply differences in flavor, but they communicate underlying beliefs about the role of corporate prayer in worship.

Congregations in which clergy always lead the prayers understand intercession to be a priestly function. Often in these settings the sharing of Holy Communion is not a weekly expectation, and thus the weekly prayer becomes the liturgical space for presiding over shared life and openness to receiving God's blessing. It is the space where the pastor tends and shepherds the congregation and draws them into communion with God, even on weeks when bread and cup are not offered. Many

United Methodists and Presbyterians might recognize themselves in this description.

In contrast, congregations in which laypeople lead the prayers understand intercession to be a work of the people. Often in these settings Holy Communion is shared weekly, and the priestly function centers around presiding at the table. Weekly Eucharist shapes the role of priest in worship, and intercessions call forth the gifts of the congregation. The priest still has a role in prayer and may offer the concluding collect to the intercessions; the difference is that the priest's role centers on a particular prayer, the Eucharistic Prayer, known as the Great Thanksgiving. Many congregations, including many Episcopalians and Lutherans, might place themselves in this category.

Another immediately noticeable difference is the name given to intercessory prayer from one church to the next. This book uses "prayers of the people" and "intercession" to refer to the same part of the liturgy. Intercession is what the person leading prayers is doing, while Prayers of the People names a specific element of the worship service, as would be printed in an order of worship or bulletin. In some traditions, they also are known as "prayers of intercession." In practice, many know this part simply as "the prayers," and the language used here incorporates this common reference as well. This book addresses intercessory prayer in the context of a worship service. While it has application to intercessory prayer groups that meet during the week, the primary concern of this volume is leading congregational prayer. In doing so, this book seeks to distinguish congregational intercessory prayer from the pastoral prayer. There are many different types of prayer: intercession is a specific type, while, in contrast, the pastoral prayer encompasses multiple types of prayer. Intercession may be led by a layperson or clergyperson; the pastoral prayer is offered by someone who has pastoral responsibility for a congregation, most likely someone ordained.

INTERCESSION AND PASTORAL PRAYER

In many mainline churches, the model for corporate prayer in the context of worship is the pastoral prayer. This book offers an alternative to that model, rather than a criticism of it. Many of the guidelines that follow about leading intercessions can be equally well applied to leading pastoral prayers. Setting these two models of prayer alongside one another helps to identify what the work of intercession exactly is. Intercession is the practice of coming before God in openness and honesty, during which we name our tenderest human need and our deepest hope for change and transformation, in the expectation that God will confer a blessing. Such a practice, enacted together with one another in the body of Christ, is so crucial to our life with God that it becomes necessary to disentangle intercession from other good and needed forms of prayer. This book displays how interceding, in being carried out with whole heart and mind, can become not so much a duty as a joy.

The differences between composing intercessory petitions as described here and compiling a pastoral prayer are not merely about style of worship or formality of language. The pastoral prayer may mark the only time of prayer in a worship service, and therefore inevitably it seeks to say everything that needs to be said to God all at once. It has to be comprehensive. Intercessory petitions, by contrast, depend on other forms of prayer, such as confession and thanksgiving, appearing at other points in worship — as is described in detail in chapter one. Like a crisscrossing shoelace, separate intercessions depend upon there being multiple points during worship where the congregation can articulate before God the full breadth of what needs to be said; the whole service is laced together by different forms of prayer.

Thus it wouldn't work to switch from a pastoral prayer to intercessory petitions without altering other elements in the worship service. This is because these two models don't belong to the same category; they are not interchangeable parts. From a distance, they may seem symmetrical in many people's minds because when people say, "I've come to church to pray," they mean they have something to say to God or to ask of God. Largely that means intercession, for themselves or others. And whether it's a pastoral prayer or intercessory petitions, this part of the service is where people who've "come to church to pray" have the most promising opportunity to do whatever they came to do. Whether intercession takes place through petitions as described here or a pastoral prayer, the form of prayer takes its shape in relationship to other prayers that might be present in the service. And in whatever form intercession takes place, it should not duplicate, and thus undercut, any other prayers. Toward this end, the ideas offered here treat intercession as a form of prayer necessary on its own terms, vital to the life of the church, and welcomed by God, who knows our needs better than we do ourselves.

SHAPING THE PRAYERS OF THE PEOPLE

The book comes in two parts: theory and practice. Chapters 1-5 lay out some ground rules for offering intercessions in a congregational setting. Of course there are other ways. But this is a book designed to answer the question "Teach us to pray": it's useless to say, "Here are fifteen different ways of doing things." Much better to say, "Here is one way, and these are its merits, and this is how to go about it, and here are some examples of how it has been carried out." Readers will take from it what they find helpful and make their own arrangements. What's written here seeks to offer grace and joy, not a new law — still less a new rote.

Chapter one begins with an exploration of what intercessory prayer is — intended to be free of theological jargon and scriptural citations, just a simple explanation of what people who pray actually think they are doing. It then goes on to explain what intercessory prayer is and what it isn't, and uses this distinction to show how intercessions can go wrong both theologically and pastorally. This chapter also offers a straightforward distinction that tries to make clear what one is trying to do in the mood and content of intercessions, and how that, in great part, explains what kind of prayers lead the congregation to feel that something important and true has been said and done.

Chapter two proposes a shape for composing intercessions — a shape that is lodged in Anglican traditions, easy to remember, straightforward to replicate, comprehensive in its scope, and satisfying in its rhythm. The rest of the chapter suggests how to inhabit that shape and make it one's own, while being able to improvise as necessary.

Chapter three suggests ways to enhance the material one has put together by dovetailing with the rest of the service. In doing so, it locates the intercessions in relationship to other parts of the liturgy. The chapter as a whole explores how to engage creatively a range of resources, notably hymns and songs, which are already lodged in the congregation's memory and ripe for prayerful use.

Chapter four explores dimensions of congregational participation, including the use of physical space and bodily posture. It assumes prayer is not only spoken but also enacted and imagines how to do that well in a variety of worship settings. This chapter delves into how prayer is lived and embodied corporately.

Chapter five is about quality control. It deals with word choice, presentation, and aesthetic value. The chapter ends with a discussion of silence and extempore prayer, in hope that improving the practice of intercession will have the fruits of enabling individuals and congregations to rest in silence; and in hope that learning the rhythms of intercession will enable practitioners to pray extempore in ways that stimulate and inspire congregations rather than bore and intimidate them.

The second part of the book consists of three chapters of examples. The examples come from a university chapel, local congregations, and community gatherings. Chapters six and seven include intercessions in liturgical settings — the first during the seasons of Advent, Christmas, Epiphany, Lent, and Easter, the second during ordinary time. Chapter eight offers prayers spoken in more informal or occasional settings. Some were offered in explicitly interfaith gatherings, and others in settings which were not of any shared faith. This chapter illustrates how to improvise in times and places where praying well requires a thoughtful sensitivity without reducing the range of what may be said to bland generalities. All the examples in these three chapters are accompanied by brief commentaries that highlight ways the principles elucidated earlier in the book have been employed.

This book is offered in a spirit of practical liturgical ecumenism. One of us is a priest in the Church of England; the other is a United Methodist pastor. What's offered here aims to build up the church, rather than strengthen one particular tradition, and because of that it seeks not to use language that is specific to any one denomination. Likewise these insights are designed to apply to both formal worship and more relaxed settings; consequently, the language used doesn't presuppose a particular style of worship. And while it does assume a Eucharistic (or word and table) shape, it also takes for granted that such a shape can be practiced in a variety of ways. This volume isn't about a new way to pray; it searches out the deep traditions of prayer in the church beyond the common boundaries of denomination, worship style, regionality, and nationality. What it's looking for and seeking to present are the qualities of prayer that draw us into the presence of God with one another. In the end, this book is a prayer — that in word and in truth the church may draw closer, in need and expectation, to the living God.

ONE

Speaking to God for the People

T O BE IN THE PRESENCE of God is humanity's purpose and destiny. The whole Bible is concerned with humanity's creation for, shrinking from, desertion from, restoration to, and preparation for being in the presence of God. The whole of the Christian life is training for, anticipating, longing for, practicing, and enjoying the presence of God.

The name we give to consciousness of being in the presence of God is prayer. The sense of being so united with God that we are almost in God while at the same time being so aware of God that we are deeply with God is what we call communion. While this can be experienced alone or with intimate and like-minded companions, the principal place in which Christians expect to find it is in public worship, among those they have not specifically chosen, with others from whom they may personally have significant differences, in the rehearsing-again for today the story of their redemption in Christ.

Consciousness of being in the presence of God evokes many kinds of dialogue. We may be overcome by awe, holiness, wonder, amazement, joy — words that we call praise, or that, in silence, we call adoration. We may become acutely conscious of our fragility, failure, foolishness, and folly, and thus eager to embark on a verbal process of repentance, confession, and seeking forgiveness, or an active process involving gestures of penance and a quest for reconciliation. We may be flooded with thanksgiving for the gift of creation and its myriad complexity; for the grace of God in Christ, in God's utter faithfulness and wondrous love in spite of our hardheartedness and perverse estrangement, and in the resurrection promises of forgiveness and eternal life; or for all the blessings of our own lives.

But we may also find ourselves urgently aware of our own neediness, the plight of those we love and care about, and the trouble and sorrow of others whom we know only by hearsay, by news item, by stray conversation or a sense there was something deeper we could only imagine. Neediness can be bonding: a burden shared is a burden halved. There are few things more transforming than feeling your grief and sorrow has been heard, received, understood, appreciated, and delivered back to you with compassion, grace, and wisdom — even blessing. But neediness can just as easily be isolating. We've all edged away from a grieving, begging, or angry person because we feared saying something patronizing or clumsy that might make things worse or because we feared letting them get close might drain our emotions dry.

This book is about how human neediness and fragility may be (1) named before God (2) in public worship (3) in ways that acknowledge their rawness yet (4) affirm profound trust that they will be heard, received, and understood by God and ultimately (5) be delivered back as a blessing. These five dimensions together constitute public intercessory prayer.

TO THE FATHER IN THE SPIRIT
THROUGH THE SON

What happens when we pray? Christians believe God is Father, Son, and Holy Spirit. All are equally God, but each plays a different role in prayer. Prayer is a conversation between the Son and the Father in which the Holy Spirit invites the believer to participate.

Christians imagine heaven as a place where the members of the Holy Trinity are surrounded by the angels and saints in glory. The Holy Spirit is constantly bringing the prayers of the angels and saints to the Son, and the Son is constantly pleading those petitions to the Father. This is the shape of prayer.

The angels and saints are not pleading on their own behalf; they are in heaven, after all; everything that was a cause of pain or distress or regret in earlier times has been transformed into blessing, and they want for nothing for themselves. So they are constantly interceding to God on our behalf. That's why prayer is appropriately described as joining the praise of God by the angels and saints that is going on all the time.

Prayer is a conversation between the Son and the Father in which the Holy Spirit invites the believer to participate.

The ministry of the Holy Spirit is, as it has

always been, to make Jesus and all that God has given us in Jesus (sometimes called "his benefits") present to us; and to make us, in all our humble and naked folly and need, but also in our faith and longing, present to Jesus. (People sometimes wonder, "Why is the Holy Spirit needed? Why can't Jesus — who is, after all, God — simply be everywhere and always alive to our needs?" The answer is that if we believe Jesus was fully human as well as fully divine — and needed to be so in order to save us — then being fully human means being in only one place at a time: and so, after his ascension, he is in heaven and not on earth. When Jesus is present to us, for example, in the sacraments or in the reading of scripture, it is the Holy Spirit that makes him so.) The Holy Spirit's work is to take our prayers and bring them into the Father's heart — so that we may fundamentally know that nothing is more important to the Father than us and our salvation, now and for-

> Every petition is, on closer scrutiny, a plea for salvation — for safety, for healing, for reconciliation, for communion, for blessing — for all the things Christ won on the cross.

ever. And then the Holy Spirit delivers back to us the life that comes from the heart of God — not always as we want or comprehend, but always, we trust, in the long (if not the short) term, as a blessing.

Perhaps the deepest mystery is what takes place between the Son and the Father. It is common to imagine God (maybe the Father, but perhaps more commonly a non-Trinitarian distant bearded figure looking like a truculent Santa Claus) being vaguely aware of our prayers but being too sleepy, too absent, too busy, too idle, or even too vengeful to address them. But this is not a picture of the scriptural God. The God of the scriptures is definitively met in the agonized Jesus on the cross. We can't look at Jesus, mocked and pierced on Calvary, and any longer retain a notion of an absent-minded, absent-hearted God. There is a sense in which the Son who pleads with the Father on our behalf is always the Jesus we see on the cross. Because every petition is, on closer scrutiny, a plea for salvation — for safety, for healing, for reconciliation, for communion, for blessing — for all the things Christ won on the cross. So every time we pray in the power of the Spirit — every time the Holy Spirit carries our prayer to Jesus and Jesus intercedes to the Father for us, the question for the Father is the same: "How much of your ultimate glory are you going to reveal and bestow at this present moment, and how much are you going to withhold until the last day?"

We might say, in our impatience, "Why can't we just have it all *now?*

Why is the Father holding anything back? Isn't that cruel, despotic manipulation from someone who must be deriving some perverse gratification from watching on as creation groans?" It's a perfectly understandable and reasonable question. It's more or less the petition we pray in the Lord's Prayer: "Thy kingdom come . . . on earth as in heaven." But what this petition is asking for is to bring creation — time — to an end, and collapse the period between the coming of Christ and the end of all things. The fact that creation is deeply good, despite the fall, and the truth that mundane, ordinary existence is profoundly valuable and suffused with God's glory: this is what holds the Father back, because this abiding and wondrous creation is what will be swallowed up in the final coming of the kingdom, where God will be all in all.

Jesus is not asking the Father to rescue us while dooming creation; but neither is he requesting that the creation be altered leaving us unchanged. What Jesus is asking the Father is that this relationship breakdown, this ovarian cyst, this outbreak of civil war, or this sudden bereavement may be transfigured by being made integral to the story of salvation and be so touched by the hand of providence that it may become a blessing to the world and the church and be transformed from a sign of despair into a sacrament of hope.

That is the awesome process one seeks to enter when one stands up to lead prayers in public worship.

THREE KINDS OF SPEECH

Public worship is a stylized activity. Not because it's ritualized, arcane, staged, or artificial, but because it's a semi-scripted dialogue that follows certain rules that those present either know or can easily follow. There's a sense that people recognize they are "doing something" together in the presence of God and they need to act in a way that respects the common purpose.

Those leading worship — those who speak aloud in the hearing of the whole congregation — exercise three kinds of speech. The secret of leading worship is not to mix them up. These three kinds of speech direct the attention of the people and communicate the common purpose.

(1) The first kind is **speaking to God for the people.** The person adopts the role portrayed in the book of Exodus (and embodied by Zechariah at the beginning of the Gospel of Luke) of the Jewish priest who enters

the holy of holies in the Temple and comes face to face with God. While the members of the congregation are indeed present, the person leading speaks with a focus and intensity as if there were no one involved but him- or herself and God. In some traditions clergy are taught, when speaking in this mode, to spread wide their arms in a posture of "gathering" so as to indicate that they are acting as a funnel for all the people's prayers.

There are a number of moments when one person speaks to God on behalf of the people. In many traditions the minister says one or more "collects" — which, as the name indicates, are intended to gather together the congregation's prayers, and are accordingly often preceded by a period of silence. In most traditions the Great Thanksgiving said over the bread and the cup is spoken by the pastor alone, addressing God on the congregation's behalf. The intercessions, sometimes known as the Prayers of the People, take their place among these other such moments when *one person speaks to God on behalf of the people;* but what may be unique about them is that they may be led by a layperson, either a congregation member or one of the church staff in a congregational care role.[1]

(2) The second kind of speech in public worship is **speaking to the people for God.** This is a very different role. Examples of speaking to the people on God's behalf include giving the greeting, pronouncing the absolution after the confession of sins, reading scripture, preaching the sermon, and pronouncing the benediction. In very traditional liturgies, such as Roman Catholic masses following the tradition existing before the Second Vatican Council, the contrast is sometimes vividly portrayed by the priest turning eastwards when speaking to God for the people and westwards when speaking to the people for God. In this mode the person speaking assumes a confidence — and a freedom — that comes from trusting that the Holy Spirit, rather than the speaker, is doing the real communicating.

(3) The third way in which one person speaks in public worship is in **helping people speak to (or participate with) one another** — in general facilitating the process by which the members of the congregation come face to face with God and one another and enter, as participants, the mystery of God's story and promise of salvation. How and how much this happens is largely a matter of local custom, but examples to be found in most traditions include inviting people to stand, sit, or join in prayer; introducing the confession; introducing the sharing of the peace; introducing

---

1. In settings where a Pastoral Prayer is offered, the pastor offering the prayer is speaking to God for the people.

the acclamations in the Great Thanksgiving (for example, "Let us proclaim the mystery of faith . . ."), and making the announcements.

At several points in the liturgy there can be a subtle shift as the speaker slips from one mode of speech to another. For example, at the sharing of the peace, the minister flips from speaking to the people for God ("The peace of the Lord be with you") to helping the people participate with one another ("Let us offer one another signs of peace"). In some traditions the confusion of address involved in this uncomfortable shift is overcome by having a second minister give the "stage directions" that help the people speak to each other — for instance, "Let us confess . . . ," "Let us share . . . ," "Let us proclaim . . . ," and "Let us depart . . ."

It is vitally important to understand the difference between these modes of speech, to value each one for what it alone can do, and wherever possible to avoid letting them blend into one another. Why is this so significant? Because allowing them to blend into one another is a sign that something's wrong — perhaps seriously wrong. Here are some of the things that might be amiss.

Blending these forms of speech indicates, at best, that the person speaking lacks confidence either in the shape of the liturgy or in colleagues leading other parts of the service. When a person doing the greeting launches into a prayer for some things currently going on in church or world, it suggests that person doesn't trust that those issues will be adequately addressed later on in the intercessions. When a preacher starts advertising an upcoming course or social event within the sermon, it implies the preacher doesn't believe the congregation will really be listening when it comes to the announcements. When a person leading intercessions reels off a list of things for which to be thankful, it seems the intercessor doesn't feel the thanksgiving prayers elsewhere in the service are adequate to do the job.

Blending the forms of speech, at worst, represents a manipulation of the congregation or an instrumentalizing of God. The introduction of the confession of sins is not the place for an editorial comment about particular ways in which a political party or a faction within the church has behaved or betrayed or in some way disappointed the speaker: the confession has to be something the whole congregation can wholeheartedly say, and any words that inhibit some or many members from doing so are to be studiously avoided. Likewise if the sermon or intercessions turn into a manifesto for a particular initiative in church or world (which would at best belong in the announcements), they're being turned from an encounter with God to the promotion of an agenda. When news reporters say, "The bishop used his Easter sermon to . . . ," they've misunderstood the nature of a sermon. Sermons aren't a means to an end; if they're truly an encounter with God, they're an end in themselves. The particular danger with the intercessions is that the speaker confuses the role of speaking to God for the people with the opportunity to share a few personal opinions or judgments with the congregation; that is, to mix up leading worship with having coffee and sharing fellowship afterwards.

STAYING IN ROLE

Let's look in a little more detail at where intercession belongs in relation to other habitual aspects of worship.

(1) Intercession does not directly address sin. That's the role of confession and absolution. If the intercessions dwell on sin, they subtly suggest that the confession has not adequately named all that's perverse and foolish in the world, and/or that the absolution has not provided sufficient deliverance from it. In preparing prayers of intercession alongside prayers of confession, the leader of worship learns to distinguish suffering from sin. Sin is a matter for confession; pain and suffering are matters for intercession. Making these kinds of distinctions is an example of how worship offers moral training for the congregation and its leaders. Thus the intercessions are not the place to dwell on the reasons for a terrible famine, the complicity of the West in the arms trade, or any other practice that may have exacerbated the causes or consequences of the famine. Instead the intercessions are the place to focus on the pain and agony involved, and to call upon God to be present to those who suffer and empower all seeking to alleviate their plight.

(2) Intercessions are most certainly not an alternative sermon. The preacher may be dull, discourteous, distressing, or downright heretical; but the intercessions are not the place to compensate for or rectify such deficiencies. How can one tell that intercessions are turning into a sermon? When the speaker drifts away from talking to God and starts talking to the congregation. When the speaker begins to use phrases like, "May we always be mindful . . ." The word "may" is a danger sign: it's invariably a signal that the speaker is about to divert into a moralistic lecture directed towards

> **Intercessions are most certainly not an alternative sermon.**

the congregation. Not only does this cease to be intercession; even more seriously it departs from the humble attitude of acknowledging need and rapidly replaces it with a tone of superiority and self-righteousness.

The other, more significant diversion is signaled when and if the speaker ceases to address God in the second person, as "you," and begins to speak of God in the third person — as "God." When this happens the speaker can only be addressing the congregation — one never names in the third person someone whom one is at the same time addressing. It's quite common for those leading prayers to cross over from speaking to God to speaking about God — for example, "Loving God, we pray that people will come to our youth group and discover the truth of the gospel and the place of God in their lives." Here the speaker has begun by talking to God and finished by talking about God. It's a subtle, but significant, transition. If the second half of the sentence is a prayer, it's not addressed to the Christian God — for it talks about God as if God isn't being directly addressed. The speaker has changed course in mid-sentence and is no longer speaking to God but is now addressing the congregation. Though subtle, this point is fundamental to leading intercessions: the most basic aspect of speech is to remember whom you're speaking to. If prayer is consciousness of being in the presence of God, everything the speaker says and does must enhance and cherish that awareness — and certainly not confuse and divert it.

(3) Intercessions are not to be confused with the creed. They presume faith, but they come not from an ordered, articulate place of nuanced faith, but from a more primal place of profound need and awareness of our creatureliness. It's very appropriate to start a prayer by recalling what God has done — as recorded, for example, in the scriptural readings for the day: "Merciful God, in your Son we see your will to meet us in our moment of greatest need and distress; look upon your people in Somalia . . ." But as soon as it becomes a litany of what God is, and has done, and will do, then it is showing a lack of confidence that the creed has adequately done this.

(4) In just the same way, the intercessions are not the place for thanksgivings and recognitions of answered prayer. The primary way thanksgiving happens liturgically is through the Great Thanksgiving at the celebration of Eucharist. If the service is not a Eucharist or the Great Thanksgiving is not considered to be specific or personal or extensive enough, then another place in the liturgy should be identified or created where the purpose is very clearly giving thanks and rejoicing in God's blessings.

One familiar model of prayer is often known by the acronym ACTS, which stands for adoration, confession, thanksgiving, and supplication.

8

Adoration means praising God for who God is. Confession means naming particular sins and asking forgiveness. Thanksgiving means recognizing God's goodness and blessing. Supplication means petitioning God for needs by asking for God's presence or action in particular ways. Those who are familiar with this model will quickly recognize that intercessions correspond to the S (for supplication). There is nothing wrong with this model; in fact, it is helpful in distinguishing four types of prayer which absolutely should be present in worship. The key is for the elements of adoration, confession, thanksgiving, and supplication, which constitute the ACTS prayer, to be spread through the whole liturgy, not compressed into only one piece of the worship service. They each constitute distinct movements of the liturgy, and they are different forms of speech. When adoration, confession, and thanksgiving creep into the supplications, it is a sign that these elements are not given sufficient expression elsewhere in the service. To some, having supplications stand alone may feel overly direct and forward. Yet having a time of prayer devoted to intercession is the primary way the church fulfills its priestly work of naming before God the cares and concerns of the world. For those who have been trained in praying the ACTS model, it may seem altogether inappropriate to begin a prayer with intercessory petitions without, in a sense, working up to this moment. This is where the whole flow of the liturgy in word and table format must be trusted to do its work, one element at a time.

Thanksgiving can be something of an anomaly in public worship. Sin is in many instances directly addressed through a prayer of confession and a subsequent declaration of absolution. Adoration is offered in a variety of ways, often through music and song or a call to worship. Thanksgiving requires more thoughtfulness. If the worship service is a Eucharist, the Great Thanksgiving offers a helpful structure. Even so, there may be a sense that more needs to be said, specific to the setting. At a Eucharist, particular thanksgivings may the focus of the prayer that follows the sharing of Holy Communion. At a service where the Eucharist is not celebrated, prayers of thanksgiving can shrink rapidly, without that being the intention. In this situation, naming particular blessings and celebrations may fit well into the prayer offered at the reception of the offering.

Thanksgiving can seep in around the edges of the other prayers because there is a sense that this form of speech is vital to being in God's presence — yet one that doesn't always have a place to belong in the liturgy or may be present but greatly abbreviated. It's important to give thought to how thanksgiving happens, when it takes place, and how to make it resonant.

The heartfelt sense of being thankful for God's blessings goes hand in hand with the courage to petition God for mercy and grace. Some congregations dedicate a time when joys can be named aloud; in a setting that is smaller and where interpersonal interaction is part of the expectation, this can be stirring. It can be as simple as the intercessor asking the congregation as the service begins, "Is there something to celebrate today?" Or it can be as generous as the celebrant concluding the prayer following the sharing of Communion with an invitation to the congregation to name aloud the joys and blessings in their lives. In other settings, it's the responsibility of the presider to offer prayers of thanks on behalf of the whole congregation. The challenge here is to stretch beyond thanking God generally and to name specific things, pertinent to congregational life, the local community, or the wider world. Perhaps there is an opportunity to give thanks for different ministries in the church in a sequence throughout the year, or to give thanks for something during the particular week just past. Perhaps the church has hosted homeless families overnight, or led Vacation Bible School, or welcomed new members through baptism. Perhaps a peace treaty has ended a foreign war or an election has taken place without violence in a troubled country. All of these are ripe for inclusion in the prayer of thanksgiving.

The point of being so particular is not that everything must be kept tidy. The point is that the work of intercession is so vital — so central to every act of worship, so integral to the essence of human life before God — that it can't be diverted or diluted by doing other, albeit worthwhile, things, especially those that are present elsewhere in almost every act of worship anyway.

(An alternative to keeping these four types of prayer distinct is found in the Pastoral Prayer. The ACTS model is often the template for the Pastoral Prayer, integrating adoration, confession, thanksgiving, and supplication/intercession into one single focused time of prayer.)

(5) Finally, and perhaps most pertinently, the intercessions are not the announcements. They are not the place to communicate information people don't already know. If a person in the congregation or the wider community has recently died, the intercessions are not the moment for people to discover what may be distressing news. Another way needs to be found to make the information known — a newsletter, an email communication, an announcement before the service begins, or a brief statement before the intercessions themselves. This is an example of the applicability of the distinction between the third kind of speech (helping the people partici-

pate) and the first (speaking to God for the people). Similarly, it's not ideal for names of troubled or ailing people to be "on the prayer list" and thus read out week after week unless they are known to the great majority of those present. Again, a newsletter is a good way to disseminate a little bit of information about such people (and any change in their condition or crisis) from time to time.

Those leading intercessions walk a challenging path in referring to matters (such as the state of a civil war in a faraway nation) that are complex and not well understood within the congregation. To give too much information either diverts the prayer into the announcements or distracts attention from God by showing off the extensive knowledge of the intercessor; to avoid the issue or speak of it too superficially risks colluding with a narrow or willful ignorance of God's world and a lack of interest in or concern for its suffering people. But here it is worth noting an important dimension of intercession: not knowing what to say. A phrase like "Be close today to all in [the place of conflict] who don't know whom to support, whether to take up arms, and what to hope for" can often say most or all of what needs to be said.

THE DRAMA OF PRAYER

Leading intercessions may be thought of as a dialogue; it may also be identified as a moment that crystallizes human creatureliness before God. Though preachers and choirs flatter themselves that they are the center of the congregation's attention, experience testifies that most people come to church to sing hymns and offer intercessions.

For all these reasons it's appropriate to speak of the drama of prayer — the expectant hush of the time of intercession. But drama is also a helpful term in another sense. One contemporary theologian talks of theology itself as a drama.[2] He talks about three kinds of speech. The first is epic. Epic speech is the attempt to paint a broad canvas, to seek an objective standpoint, to tell a story all can identify with and endorse, to be dispassionate and balanced and judicious and even-handed. The second is lyric. Lyric is very different: it is the willingness to be passionate, involved, and

---

2. Hans Urs von Balthasar, *Theo-Drama: Theological Dramatic Theory,* 5 vols., trans. Graham Harrison (San Francisco: Ignatius Press, 1988-1998). For a summary, see Aidan Nichols, *No Bloodless Myth: A Guide through Balthasar's Dramatics* (Edinburgh: T&T Clark, 2000).

committed. It is willing to take sides, not afraid to be subjective, open to emotion, hungry for intensity and feeling. The third is dramatic. Dramatic is a synthesis of epic and lyric. It seeks the intensity of lyric but the breadth and scope of epic. Dramatic is the nature of the scriptural story and the life of the church. For example, the story of Jesus' passion blends epic and lyric to powerful effect. Peter's denial as the cock crows is lyric at its most poignant and heart-wrenching; the centurion's statement, "Truly this man was the Son of God," is a bald epic judgment. When Jesus says to Mary, "Do not cling to me, for I have not yet ascended . . . ," it is an unforgettable dramatic interweaving of lyric and epic, because Mary's grief and longing for closeness are as present in the story as Jesus' conquest of death.

Those leading intercessions — speaking back to God the people's need in the light of God's story — are attempting a similar dramatic synthesis. They are placing our own lyric suffering and apprehension in the light of the epic landscape of God's providence; and they are setting the lyric plight of peoples near and far in the context of an epic sense of the well-being of the world — even the universe — as a whole. It is this interplay of intense, personal, urgent need and larger, broader civilization and providence that makes prayers so hard to prepare but so vital to the congregation's sense of its place in the world and in God's purposes. Get it wrong, and the congregation may be left feeling parochial and self-absorbed (if too lyric) or impersonal and uninvolved (if too epic). Get it right, and those present may be inspired — however grim the subjects mentioned — by their place in the kingdom and God's concern even for the hairs on their heads.

A Time-Honored Shape

THE COLLECT

ONE KIND OF PRAYER THAT goes back through more than a millennium of Christian worship, and has been particularly refined and cherished in the Anglican and Episcopal tradition, is the collect. When we bow to worship we know not what best to say or how rightly to say it. The collect literally *collects* the disparate and disjointed hopes and fears of all the years and renders them into phrases with which we can learn the habit of addressing God.

In the sixteenth century Archbishop of Canterbury Thomas Cranmer, charged with turning the largely clerical and monastic prayer of the church into prayer for the English common people in their own language, fell back on the great prayers of the Roman church going back to papal collections of the fifth and sixth centuries — prayers that themselves imitate the Psalms, the great prayer- and hymn-book of the church. Cranmer translated and reinvigorated these prayers and gave to the Anglican Communion one of its most precious and enduring treasures — a treasure that many other traditions have adopted and adapted. There is a collect for every Sunday of the year, and that collect is usually read at each service throughout the week that follows. There are additional collects for saints' days and special commemorations such as Ash Wednesday and Ascension Day. Perhaps one of the best known across denominations is the collect for purity, which goes like this:

Almighty God,
to whom all hearts are open, all desires known, and from whom no secrets
　　are hidden:
cleanse the thoughts of our hearts by the inspiration of your Holy Spirit,
　　that we may perfectly love you, and worthily magnify your holy name;
　　through Christ our Lord. Amen.[1]

This type of prayer may be divided into five constituent elements.

1. There is, first of all, the address to God: "Almighty God." Collects always begin by naming the one to whom they are addressed, for whose ears they are intended.

2. They then proceed to name a context in which God has been active, and thus identify the reason why the person praying has reason to trust that God will listen and respond to her or his petition: "to whom all hearts are open, all desires known, and from whom no secrets are hidden."

3. Next they offer the petition itself — what precisely the speaker pleads with God to do: "cleanse the thoughts of our hearts by the inspiration of your Holy Spirit."

4. Usually, though not always, they proceed to describe the outcome the speaker imagines, often in terms of the change to the speaker him- or herself and to the community: "that we may perfectly love you, and worthily magnify your holy name."

5. The conclusion comes with the shaping of the prayer in the light of the Trinitarian communication described in chapter one above. The ministry of the Holy Spirit is sometimes, but not always, mentioned, but the action of Christ in interceding to the Father almost always is: "through Christ our Lord." The traditional ending to many collects is left out of the 1662 Prayer Book, but that is probably because it was so widely used it didn't need including. It goes like this: "through Jesus Christ your Son our Lord, who is alive and reigns with you in the unity

---

1. The Collect for Purity appears in Episcopal, Lutheran (ELCA), Presbyterian (PC[USA]) and Methodist (United Methodist) liturgies as an opening prayer in worship including Holy Communion. *The Book of Common Prayer* (New York: Church Publishing Corp., 1979), pp. 323, 355. *Evangelical Lutheran Worship* (Minneapolis: Augsburg Fortress Press, 2006), p. 95. *Book of Common Worship* (Louisville: Westminster John Knox Press, 1993), p. 50. *United Methodist Book of Worship* (Nashville: The United Methodist Publishing House, 1992), p. 6.

of the Holy Spirit, one God, now and forever." The prayer finishes with the traditional ending to all Christian prayers: "Amen."[2]

It is illuminating to take many of the well-known collects and in this way break them down into their constituent elements. Here, for example, is a familiar collect found in morning prayer in both Lutheran and Presbyterian traditions:

1. Eternal God,
2. you call us to ventures
   of which we cannot see the ending,
   by paths as yet untrodden,
   through perils unknown.
3. Give us faith to go out with courage,
   not knowing where we go,
4. but only that your hand is leading us,
   and your love supporting us;
5. through Jesus Christ our Lord. Amen.[3]

And a collect for Ash Wednesday in the United Methodist tradition:

1. O God,
2. maker of everything and judge of all that you have made, from the dust of the earth you have formed us and from the dust of the earth you would raise us up.
3. By the redemptive power of the cross, create in us clean hearts and put within us a new spirit,
4. that we may repent of our sins and lead lives worthy of your calling;
5. through Jesus Christ our Lord. Amen.[4]

---

2. C. Frederick Barbee and Paul F. M. Zahl, in *The Collects of Thomas Cranmer* (Grand Rapids: Wm. B. Eerdmans Publishing Co., 2006), offer a very helpful understanding of the collect, including setting out the structure of a collect as presented here.

3. *Evangelical Lutheran Worship*, p. 304. *Book of Common Worship*, p. 501. It is debatable whether this last collect has a true fourth element or whether what's identified here as (4) is really an expansion of (3). This is an example where the line between the petition (3) and the outcome (4) is not clear because the petition and the outcome overlap. While this is an exception to the norm, the fourth element does not appear distinctly in every collect.

4. Laurence Hull Stookey, *The United Methodist Hymnal* (Nashville: The United Methodist Publishing House, 1989), p. 353.

And a collect for the season following Pentecost found in both Lutheran and Episcopal worship:

1. Almighty and everlasting God,
2. you are always more ready to hear than we to pray, and to give more than we either desire or deserve:
3. Pour upon us the abundance of your mercy,
4. forgiving us those things of which our conscience is afraid, and giving us those good things for which we are not worthy to ask, except through the merits and mediation of Jesus Christ our Savior;
5. who lives and reigns with you and the Holy Spirit, one God, forever and ever. Amen.[5]

And here is a collect for guidance from the Episcopal Church:

1. Heavenly Father,
2. in you we live and move and have our being:
3. We humbly pray you so to guide and govern us by your Holy Spirit,
4. that in all the cares and occupations of our life we may not forget you, but may remember that we are ever walking in your sight;
5. through Jesus our Lord. Amen.[6]

And finally a concluding collect for the Prayers of the People in Presbyterian worship:

1. Merciful God,
2. as a potter fashions a vessel from humble clay,
   you form us into a new creation.
3. Shape us, day by day,
   through the cross of Christ your Son,
4. until we pray as continually as we breathe
   and all our acts are prayer;
5. Through Jesus Christ
   and in the mystery of the Holy Spirit, we pray. Amen.[7]

---

5. *The Book of Common Prayer,* p. 234 (Proper 22). *Lutheran Book of Worship* (Minneapolis: Augsburg Publishing House, 1978), p. 26 (Twelfth Sunday after Pentecost).

6. *The Book of Common Prayer,* p. 100.

7. *Book of Common Worship,* p. 108.

There are many ways of structuring intercessions; but it is good to make this structure the song of your heart, because of its simplicity, elegance, comprehensiveness, flexibility, and adaptability to almost any circumstance. It avoids every one of the pitfalls enumerated in the previous chapter and addresses the precise needs of intercessory prayer: that it be focused on God, the Holy Trinity; that it be mindful of what God has already done that makes the request more plausible and appropriate; that it be direct in what it is seeking God to do; that it have some notion of the desired outcome and of the change in the believer that may be required for or consequent upon this outcome; and that it be conscious of what happens within God as we pray. It can do all those things in just a few words. It's not clear that anything else can.

This chapter shall therefore examine what it means to compose intercessory prayers according to this time-honored shape.

ADDRESSING GOD

Who does the person praying think God is? The previous chapter explored the "lyric" notion of God as our intimate, passionate, tender companion and the "epic" notion of God as almighty, immutable, eternal, and all-knowing. Intercessory prayer is looking for a "dramatic" synthesis of the two.

Part of addressing God is a proper fear of God. God knows those interceding better than they know themselves; that evokes a proper fear in a lyric sense — that no secrets are hid. And God is far beyond what they desire or deserve; that evokes an epic fear, a fear that the universe and God's purposes are above and outside us. Together these constitute a truly godly fear.

God, and the disciple's relationship with God, must be lyric, because those praying must genuinely believe that God knows their deepest desires better than they do and loves them better than they love themselves. If intercession becomes an anxious attempt to list exhaustively every concern of personal, local, and global significance, it stops being a joy and a relief and quickly becomes a burden and a curse. God knows what's on believers' hearts before they pray. It's not a memory test.

But God must also be epic — for God's vision and purpose stretch way beyond imagination or conception, and they include places and peoples far outside the intercessor's compass. If God is simply one's best friend, one may receive comfort and security but one misses out on awe and wonder. The glory of God is both that one has been made party to the nature and destiny of the universe and that that nature and destiny have become present in human form and are among us now in the ministry of the Holy Spirit.

So if every prayer begins with language such as "Eternal God" or "Almighty and everlasting Lord" there is an assumption that God is primarily or wholly epic — in control, yes, but somewhat distant and detached. Yet if prayers restrict their beginnings to phrases such as "Loving Father" or "Tender God," they may be in danger of going to the other extreme and portraying God in lyric terms to the exclusion of a wider frame of reference.

If one is aiming for the intercessions to last four to five minutes, and if one adopts the pattern of the collect commended in this chapter, then one is looking to prepare perhaps four petitions, followed by a concluding prayer. It's ideal if these four petitions each address God; and it's important that their forms of address represent a range of language and imagery for God, including feminine imagery. The aspiration should be that our ways of addressing God should be at least as diverse as those found in scripture. The Bible includes well over a hundred names for God: just to illustrate with the letter *a,* we find, among others, Advocate, Almighty, Anointed, Apostle, Author and Perfecter of our faith, Alpha and Omega. It should be possible to go for several weeks without using the same name twice. The names used shouldn't be so eye-catching that they distract the congregation from the task in hand; but this is a wonderful opportunity to reflect diversity in addressing God — perhaps the most direct way in which people's wide variety of knowing and encountering God can be liturgically expressed — and the chance should not be missed.

Our ways of addressing God should be at least as diverse as those found in scripture.

Having four petitions offers a way of balancing the challenging and the familiar. It also provides an invitation to choose corresponding forms of address to begin each petition, for example, "Loving God . . . ," "Desiring God . . . ," "Yearning God . . . ," "Delivering God. . . ." One way of doing this is to pick up a selection of related themes from a familiar prayer or hymn; for example, on Advent Sunday it may work well to adapt the invocations of the hymn "O come, O come, Emmanuel," and begin successive petitions "O Rod of Jesse," "O Dayspring," "O Key of David," and so on — and likewise perhaps to base the petition itself around the words of each respective verse.

It is normal, as we discussed in chapter one, to address prayers to the Father, through the Son, in the Holy Spirit. Jesus called his Father "Abba"

18

— an affectionate form of address. Employing the traditional language of "Father" preserves the dramatic combination of epic and lyric, and meanwhile, even more importantly, preserves the Christian notion of salvation as something brought about in the mystery of Jesus' relationship with the Father. But "Father" does not exhaust the Christian imagination concerning the first person of the Trinity and the direction of intercessory prayer. Long before feminism alerted the church to the way the dominance of male imagery can be restrictive for all and damaging for some, mystics and exegetes and theologians had become accustomed to addressing God in a wider range of terms. "Creator" is appropriate but somewhat limited, being impersonal; "Mother" is to be found in scripture and especially in saints such as Julian of Norwich, but is always in danger of simply swinging the pendulum in the opposite direction; "Fountain of Grace" and "Joy of Our Desiring" convey vivid, compelling imagery that isn't specifically personal but is dynamic and allusive in helpful ways.

And it is not always necessary to address prayers to the first person of the Trinity. It is perfectly possible, and theologically appropriate, to call upon Jesus, particularly in times of visceral need, and assume he will "do the rest." The thief on the cross says to Jesus, "Jesus, remember me when you come into your kingdom" (Luke 23:42); this is undoubtedly an intercessory prayer — indeed, it is the only time in the Gospels a person calls on Jesus directly without attaching some title such as "Son of David." But how timely — and what an inspiration to us, that, in our moment of most profound need, when we feel like that thief, we can simply address Jesus directly and let Jesus sort out the Trinitarian relations that lead to our prayer being answered.

One may ask, "Why not just pray to Jesus every time? Why bring the Father and the Holy Spirit into it?" Because Jesus taught us to pray to the Father in his name; but also, to respect the Trinitarian shape of God is to remind ourselves that Jesus is not a slot machine into which we shove our petition and from which we expect to receive, reasonably often, a jackpot. To pray is to enter the mystery of the relation of the Father and the Son, which is a profound occasion of awe and wonder, regardless of the outcome of our prayers. Praying is worth doing for its own sake. It's entering an eternal dance of love. It's not, except in cases of dire urgency, simply a case of putting our list of demands on the table and getting back to whatever else we were doing.

The only risk about altering the habit of praying to the Father through the Son in the Spirit is getting in a tangle and losing track of which member of the Trinity you're addressing. The person interceding on behalf of the congregation is supposed to be making it easier for the people to pray — not harder; and if the person of the Trinity being addressed is unclear or confused, it can have a distressing and troubling effect on the members of the congregation. The person leading prayers should be modeling how to pray so that the people participating both sense, and are inspired to imitate, the way prayer orders our personal and common lives before God. There should be a sense of liberation that now, at last, after a helter-skelter week, all is ordered so that after interceding together it is much clearer what lies for me to do, what burdens I share (in a way that makes them halved) with my community, and what I can safely leave with God. Getting the address to God in a muddle inhibits that transforming process. That's why it's usually best to stick to a regular pattern.

Becoming clearer about who God is and how God acts helps us become clearer about what we want or need God to do.

The underlying problem that leads to getting in a tangle isn't usually about what may sound like a rather precious preoccupation with the respective roles of the persons of the Trinity. Much more often the real problem is that the speaker isn't entirely sure what he or she is actually seeking for God to do and what outcome is actually imagined (sections 3 and 4 in the outline of a collect above). Becoming clearer about what we want or need God to do helps us become clearer about who God is and how God acts; and the opposite is equally true — becoming clearer about who God is and how God acts helps us become clearer about what we want or need God to do.

BEING ROOTED IN SCRIPTURE

And so to the second section of the prayer. Intercession is based on hope: hope that God will hear, listen, understand better than the members of the congregation do themselves, and act in tangible ways. Hope is itself based on memory. The intercessor believes God will act because the intercessor believes God has acted before. Israel called upon God to act in the Babylonian exile and based that hope on the memory that God had acted in bringing Israel out of Egyptian slavery many centuries before. So this second movement in the prayer reminds both God and those gathered for worship that they are resuming a relationship that's already in full swing. This is not a cry in the wilderness — it's an appeal for God to keep to a track record and act in character.

When intercession is part of a conventional liturgical service, like Sunday worship or Holy Communion, the simplest way to affirm this is to take cues from the readings set or chosen for the day. A straightforward way to prepare is to make a copy of the two or three readings assigned and underline a handful of key phrases that stand out or resonate as you ponder and meditate upon them several times. You can then write out three or four of these resonant phrases and see whether it's possible to group together, under the respective headings, most or all of the most pressing concerns of world and church and community.

Let's imagine you are preparing intercessions for Pentecost Sunday and the readings for the day include the story of the Tower of Babel in Genesis 11 and the account of the coming of the Holy Spirit in tongues of fire in Acts 2. As you survey Genesis 11:1-9 you pick out the following phrases:

"Let us make a name for ourselves"

So the Lord scattered them abroad from there over the face of all the earth

"Let us go down, and confuse their language there, so that they will not understand one another's speech"

Therefore it was called Babel, because there the Lord confused the language of all the earth

And as you survey Acts 2:2-21 you identify the following phrases:

There came a sound like the rush of a violent wind

Tongues, as of fire, appeared among them

All of them were filled with the Holy Spirit and began to speak in other languages

"In our own languages we hear them speaking about God's deeds of power"

"Everyone who calls on the name of the Lord shall be saved"

Then you look at those phrases a second time in the light of the global, church, and community concerns that are in the news and on people's hearts and minds as they come to worship. Let's imagine there's been some kind of conflict or instability in Iraq, where the ancient Babel (perhaps Babylon) is usually understood to be located. And let's suppose that there has been some intense dissent or development within the European Union; and meanwhile a tornado in one region of the United States. Thus you can start to group matters concerning Iraq, and perhaps wider concerns in the Middle East under the heading of "Babel"; issues in Europe and perhaps other more general international and intercultural themes under the heading of "in our languages we hear them speaking about God's power"; and casualties of the tornado under the heading of "a sound like the rush of a violent wind."

Now you have three petitions beginning to emerge. The first one might begin like this:

God of city and desert

at Babel you confused the people who sought to make a name for themselves that was not derived from your holy name;

visit your children who find themselves in Babel today, trying in Iraq to make a new country amid the confusion of languages and faiths and cultures and political alignments. . . .

While the second petition might start as follows:

God of mountain and plain,

at Pentecost the people gathered in Jerusalem heard your Son's disciples speaking in their own languages about your deeds of power;

gather the leaders of the European peoples around the desire to speak your language; send your Holy Spirit to those in [a particular country or region] and elsewhere who are bitterly and violently divided because of different cultures, languages, and histories. . . .

And the third petition might open thus:

God of wind and fire,

when you sent your Holy Spirit among the disciples you did so in dazzling tongues and astonishing gusts;

look with mercy on your people who this week have experienced tornado and whirlwind, and all whose plans for the future have been suddenly and shockingly torn apart or blown away. . . .

The secret is not to look for exact correspondences, still less prophecies or words of doom, but to find phrases that are full of resonance and heavy with multiple applications. The phrases should open up a field of concern, rather than determine an agenda: after all, the mood of intercession is compassion and mercy, rather than teaching and discipline. For example, if the reading has included the words, "What God has joined together, let no one separate," the corresponding prayer might begin, "Constant God, in your Son you declared your purpose for lifelong covenant love; be close to all who search for that love today . . ." The prayer may then go on to incorporate both those who search for a companion to share their days and those who are struggling truly to be a companion to the one with whom they do share their days. "Teach us to keep our marriage vows and show the wayward the way of your truth" isn't really a prayer — rather it's a lecture disguised as a prayer, and an exclusive lecture directed only at those who are married.

> **The secret is to find phrases that are full of resonance and heavy with multiple applications.**

It is perfectly possible to include at this moment words of a well-known hymn or prayer, particularly — as on a major festival, such as Christmas or Easter, when the hymns for the day are practically known by heart by many of those present. But it is still desirable to refer directly to scripture, in order to affirm that the Christian knowledge of and trust in God is first and fundamentally derived from the Bible.

It is not necessary to avoid the "difficult" passages. Quite the contrary. It is liberating for the congregation for the intercessor to inhabit the most challenging parts of scripture and model how such passages can become doors to honesty and truth. One particular way in which this can happen is through lament. Lament is the practice — widespread in the Bible — of naming a subject of pain or grief, making explicit just how damaging it is, and turning to God both in protest and, at the same time, in humble recognition that only

God can address it, while profoundly underlining a conviction that God truly will visit and redeem the faithful in due time. Thus the protest identifies the underlying — but troublingly hidden — reality. The Psalms are full of such cases. Here are the opening two verses of Psalm 13: "How long, O Lord? Will you forget me forever? How long will you hide your face from me? How long must I bear pain in my soul, and have sorrow in my heart all day long? How long shall my enemy be exalted over me?" These make perfect material for intercession, since they articulate both need and expectation. Thus one may pray, "God of justice and mercy, your Psalms speak of your people's longing to see your face and to know your presence among them; visit us today in our time of desperate need; come among us at this moment of crisis and despair; and show us who you are and who we truly are. . . ." At a time of disaster or shame in a community, such words speak of all hope being founded on God.

Passages that are hard to preach on come into their own in intercessory prayer. Take for example the story in 1 Samuel 15 where Saul fails to carry out God's instructions, which were as follows: "Go and attack Amalek, and utterly destroy all that they have; do not spare them, but kill both man and woman, child and infant, ox and sheep, camel and donkey" (v. 3). This is a story lectionaries tend to steer clear of (although it's not possible to understand the story of David, let alone the book of Esther, without an awareness of this crucial moment when God turned decisively against Saul). This story may become intercession like this: "Leading and guiding God, your servant Saul turned aside from your instruction in time of war; send your Holy Spirit on all who find themselves in the midst of hatred and battle; give wisdom to any who don't know whether to follow instruction or change course in the heat of the moment; and show your face to those who find the letter of your law to be in conflict with their understanding of your nature and grace. . . ."

The following notorious verses in Psalm 137 (vv. 8-9) may provide a further example: "O daughter Babylon, you devastator! Happy shall they be who pay you back what you have done to us! Happy shall they be who take your little ones and dash them against the rock!" These verses are invariably edited out when this psalm is read in a worship service. But an intercessor may employ them thus: "God of all things and all peoples, your Psalms tell us of the bitterness of your people in the face of injustice and defeat; work in the hearts of all who nurse hatred; be close to all who are so stirred to violent revenge that they lose sight of everything else; and teach each one of us the paths of your peace, even when those ways pass our understanding. . . ."

In such ways not only does scripture shape prayer, but prayer informs and even redeems the way the church reads scripture.

24

DARING TO BE IMPERATIVE

Intercession is looking to God in need and expectation. These are the words of Jesus on which intercessory prayer is founded: "Ask, and it will be given you; search, and you will find; knock, and the door will be opened for you. For everyone who asks receives, and everyone who searches finds, and for everyone who knocks, the door will be opened. Is there anyone among you who, if your child asks for bread, will give a stone? Or if the child asks for a fish, will give a snake? If you then, who are evil, know how to give good gifts to your children, how much more will your Father in heaven give good things to those who ask him!" (Matt. 7:7-11). Ask . . . seek . . . knock: these are the dimensions of intercession.

This is not the moment for inhibition or respectful silence. God is not too busy, too distant, or too important to attend to our prayers. On the contrary, there's nothing God wants more than for us to bring our need and expectation to the heart of the Trinity. So it is crucial that we ask — in words of one syllable. This means using imperative verbs. "Give . . . visit . . . come among . . . save . . . defend . . . uphold . . . inspire": this is the language of scriptural hope.

Let's start by considering the way prayers are often articulated. It's common to think of intercessions, private and public, as a laundry list. "We pray for the President, we pray for the bishop, we pray for our elected representatives, we pray for the Middle East, we pray for the poor. . . ." Now, let's be clear: to pray in this way is infinitely better than not to pray at all. But does it honor the instruction, "Ask, and it will be given you; search, and you will find; knock, and the door will be opened for you"? It seems to require very little of us and to expect very little of God. Indeed, the emphasis seems somewhat less on the God who does the listening than on we who do the praying. It's in the indicative — describing an action: "We pray for. . . ." It's tempting to say, "Go on, *pray* then — don't just talk about the fact that you're doing so." (One particularly unfortunate liturgical form of intercession begins each petition with the words, "I ask your prayers for. . . ." This turns prayer on its head by making the intercessor speak to the congregation and not to God, thus deferring the moment of intercession until the silence that follows each petition.)

What's missing here is quite simple: an imperative verb. The question is, "What *precisely* do you want God to do?" This takes a little thought: but such forethought is exactly what a congregation has every reason to expect from the person leading the prayers. It's worth mapping out the kind of things we might wish God to do.

- When a person, or a group of people, is in deep trouble, the prayer is uncomplicated. If miners are stuck below ground, or a little child is missing, presumed abducted, we simply ask God — "save . . . find. . . ." Hence we say, "Guide the hand of those searching for [name], and bring hope and comfort to her family, friends. and neighbors." The important thing here is, in a lyric way, to touch the level of emotion involved.

- When a country or continent is facing economic crisis, the prayer is a little more subtle. If unemployment or inflation figures are terrible, we need to balance our awareness that some people are particularly influential while others might be most deeply affected. Thus we might say, "Be close to the people of [region or country]; surround those without work, money, or prospects, with friends, kindness, and resilience; and give wisdom and compassion to all charged with restoring economic confidence and growth." The vital thing in this case is to address the issue from various perspectives without turning it into a newspaper editorial.

- When a person within the congregation is in a time of transition or need, the prayer needs to be finely judged. This isn't a tribute speech or a passing-on of pastoral insight. Hence we might say, "Bless [name] as she comes to an end of her time at Graystone Memorial; give her everything she needs to complete her time in this community to your honor and glory; and put hope in her heart as she faces the work you have in store for her at St. Gabriel's." It's not for the intercessor to judge whether she has been a profound blessing to the Graystone Memorial community or not; that's not a matter for prayer. What is a matter for prayer is to seek God's blessing on her ending, transition, and new beginning. Again, the secret is to remember the speaker is talking to God, and not to the congregation.

- There will always be times when it's hard to know how to pray or what to pray for. It's important intercessors don't show off their extensive knowledge of foreign affairs: that simply distracts attention from God to themselves. Naming a variety of points of view shows suitable compassion and concern. Remembering anniversaries is one such sign of faithfulness and memory. Thus "Be close to the people of Haiti [x] years after the earthquake. Strengthen the hand of all seeking to rebuild homes, relationships, and livelihoods; comfort any whose grief

26

is overwhelming; and show your face to those who wonder where they can find you."

What do we really want God to do? What are the verbs that articulate the action of God that we are genuinely looking for? We may gather those intentions around three definitive moments of revelation in Christ: resurrection, transfiguration, and incarnation.

1. *Resurrection.* This is where we want God to bring about change, through miracle, through a reversal of events, through bringing about the unlikely, the amazing, the unexpected. South Africa moved to majority rule without widespread violence: so maybe other countries may do so. September 11 was not followed by a dozen or a hundred such attacks: so maybe a world overshadowed by terror is not inevitable.

There are three kinds of problems in the world: those arising from the contingency and mortality of creation; those stemming from human ignorance, folly, carelessness, pride, and lack of faith; and those attributable to genuine malevolence and evil intent. It's helpful to pray differently in each circumstance — recognizing that sometimes more than one may be involved.

- Malevolence (such as an oppressive regime). Change the hearts of those in power. . . . Strengthen those who are resisting the attacks. . . . Bring to justice every person who has. . . .

- Folly (such as global warming, neglect of the vulnerable). Give wisdom. . . . Raise up leaders who. . . . Bring to faith. . . .

- Contingency (such as earthquake, cancer). Strengthen all who seek to help. . . . Bring healing. . . . Hold back the winds and waves. . . .

It's a subtle but important point that we don't call God's actions "interventions" or "interventions in history." The universe belongs to God: acting in the universe is God's prerogative. The language of God's "intervention" suggests, by contrast, that the world is ours, and that God occasionally "intervenes" in a story that is otherwise always about us. Such interventions thus almost inevitably seem arbitrary. The truth is otherwise. God's action is the norm. Our life — our time on this planet — is the interruption, often an unhelpful one.

27

2. *Transfiguration.* The hymn (based on Psalm 67) crystallizes this second mode of prayer: "God of mercy, God of grace, Show the brightness of Thy face; Shine upon us, Savior, shine, Fill Thy Church with light divine."

So long as intercessions lead with imperative verbs, they usually take an active, helpful, dynamic shape.

This refers to situations where miracle is not what's required — or where the change that's sought is too complex to articulate briefly or publicly. Perhaps the prayer is for insight or wisdom or understanding amidst confounding circumstances. Or maybe the prayer is that the person would see him- or herself as God sees that person, made in God's image. Such a case may be the person facing a terminal illness — "Shine your face upon Julia and let her see your glory." Another such context may be the beginning of a new ministry — "Give David hope and joy and reveal your power and purpose in his life."

We may think of this category as the default mode of intercessory prayer — where there isn't necessarily something profoundly wrong, and yet we are called to remember people before God at a particular season or significant moment in their lives.

3. *Incarnation.* This is the most basic prayer, where we don't know what exactly to say, but we seek the most fundamental form of God's response — presence. We don't know details, we don't want to make judgments, or perhaps it's not appropriate to disclose information. A divorce is in process, legal proceedings are afoot, a journey with an eating disorder or substance addiction seems endless, a civil war has gone on as long as anyone can remember. Here we say, "Be with the people of. . . . Bless all who struggle with. . . . Be close to any who suffer from. . . . Send your Holy Spirit upon those who. . . ."

So long as intercessions lead with imperative verbs, they usually take an active, helpful, dynamic shape.

One place where intercessions can get into a tangle is when it comes to those who have died. The bland, catch-all "We pray for [name] . . ." is not especially helpful here. It's possible to discern three categories of people that may be in mind:

1. Those well-known to the congregation. Here the prayer is like a funeral prayer: "As you kept [name] close to you throughout his life, keep him

in your heart now and forever" — to be accompanied by prayers for the bereaved, by name if possible.

2. Those not generally known, but whose names have appeared on a prayer list of some kind. Because the circumstances are not common knowledge, only a general prayer is possible: thus, "Lord, in you nothing is wasted: as you took the loaves and fishes and made an abundant banquet, take these lives and transform them into glory in your eternal kingdom."

3. Those who are completely unknown but are at the center of public attention, having died in a major disaster such as a hurricane. Here it is best to stick to very broad generalities: "Have mercy on your people in distress, bind up the wounded, comfort the bereaved, and take the departed into your loving arms. ..." To offer such a prayer isn't to make a definitive statement about eternal salvation: members of the congregation may differ, for example, in their understandings of the ultimate fate of the unbeliever. To entrust the dead to the everlasting mercy of God is simply to hope and seek the best for them while leaving judgment to God, which is all we can do for anybody.

There's something about such prayers — particularly in the face of tragedy — that has a strong tendency to lose sight of the subject, object, and purpose of the prayer. Thus it's not uncommon for the person speaking to say something like, "Our hearts go out to the people in ..." — somewhat echoing the language of public expressions of compassion and solidarity. These are noble and no doubt genuine sentiments — but they are not an intercessory prayer. They draw attention to our own feelings rather than another's need, and they are very vague about what the prayer is actually asking God to do. The reason for stressing this point is that this is precisely the moment when the congregation needs the intercessor to disentangle strong feelings and confused desires — rather than mimic or echo them. The intercessor does the congregation a huge service by identifying the kinds of people involved ("members of the emergency services, relief teams, those searching desperately for loved ones, all trying to make contact from afar ...") and by naming what we are looking to God to do ("comfort ... give strength ... sustain ... offer life ... empower ... bring hope ... shed mercy ...").

Another delicate area is praying for the sick. When people are invited to name those on their hearts and minds, whether during a service (perhaps in a time for sharing aloud or alternatively in a side chapel) or more informally (for example in a home group), illness is by far the most common thing mentioned. Recovery of health, while of course central to the concerns of so many people so much of the time, somehow has the status of the most legitimate and respectable thing to pray for.

Here the delicacy is the invariably confidential nature of the precise condition and prognosis of the person suffering. No one is going to say aloud in public the words, "Help Marjorie and her family come to terms with the fact that her death is near, and give them grace to have the conversations with one another that are currently being obscured by the need to keep her cheerful and be unrealistically positive." But many people will be praying such words in the silence of their hearts; the point is to convey much of the character of such insights in ways that concentrate on petition to God rather than social commentary. Likewise, no one is likely to say, "God of mercy, Claire died only nine months ago with that wretched husband of hers at the wheel and now her eldest daughter has this terrible wasting illness: how can you in your providential love possibly allow one family to go through such grief? Come down now and deliver them and show them your face and uphold them in their agony and dismay." But again that may be exactly what many congregation members are thinking, and the closer the intercessor can get to the lyric quality of these sentiments — without pointing the finger at the "wretched husband" — the better.

Many parish churches keep prayer lists of the sick. These lose credibility the more they drift away from congregational relationship, regular trimming, and genuine dialogue with the persons in question. Listing a dozen or more stand-alone names is not particularly worshipful. Much better — and straightforward, now that such lists can be updated electronically — is that the contact person be listed in brackets beside the person to be prayed for, and that that contact person be asked (in advance, in writing) to offer a form of words appropriate to the person's circumstances: "give her hope as she awaits a diagnosis"; "comfort them in their time of loss"; "give him strength as he lives with cancer"; "show her your face and empower her medical support team as she struggles with constant discomfort."

The harder the intercessor works to articulate exactly who is being prayed for and precisely what God is being asked to do, the more the congregation will have a liberating sense that transformational prayer is taking place.

Depending upon the size of the congregation and the length of the prayer list, names on such a list can be distributed among the worshipers for particular intercessions during worship. If each name on the prayer list is printed on a laminated card and placed in a basket, the names (and whatever information is available about specific needs) can be easily distributed among the congregation. Each worshiper then has the opportunity to remember a particular person from the list during a time of silence in the intercessions. The names can be collected after the service and subsequently redistributed the next week. Over time, this deepens connections within the congregation as parishioners pray specifically for one another, and it serves as an alternative to reading through the full prayer list each week. The intercessor might open this petition and the silence that follows with, "Lord God, in your Son you brought us the comfort of being yoked to you when our cares grow heavy. Yoke us, one with another, in seeking your compassion and gentle leading. In silence, we bring before those on our prayer list whose lives are heavy with cares."

MAKING SUBORDINATE PETITIONS

If each petition is based on the model of a collect, it's usually best to restrict public intercessions in regular liturgical worship to three or four petitions. A script of four hundred to four hundred-fifty words is the most that a typical congregation can absorb.

The secret is, rather than take on too many subjects, to see the interrelatedness and depth of the few subjects it is possible to cover. The building up of subordinate petitions, related to but dovetailing with the main focus of the prayer, enriches and expands the sense of waiting on God and meditating on the scripture. For example, if one of the scripture passages for the day is Elijah and the widow at Zarephath, then a spiral of themes can develop, starting with hunger, moving to those who grow and produce food, and moving to issues of disordered eating, as follows:

1. God of abundance,

2. Your prophet Elijah came to the widow in a time of famine;

3. Visit today the people of X and Y; empower all who grow crops and rear livestock there, and strengthen the hand of those who bring supplies and expertise from outside the region. Work in the lives of all who work in the food service industry — in factories, distribution centers, supermarkets, local shops, cafes, and restaurants. Be close to any in Z or in this city who

go to bed hungry tonight; and send your Holy Spirit on all for whom food
and body-image are a source of fear, shame, denial, or pain.

4. Make us a people for whom food is a sign of your faithfulness and a
token of your sacrificial love for us in your Son.

5. Lord, in your mercy. . . .

Consider for a moment just how many things are taking place in a prayer
of this kind.

- A statement is being made in the language used to address God. Here
that gesture is a bold one — speaking, in the context of hunger and
scarcity, of God's inherent abundance that is always more than enough,
an abundance that is not diminished by human contingency, folly, or
malevolence.

- The scripture is no longer a story from long ago and far away, but becomes a catalyst for transformative understanding, renewed hope, and
a plea for the action of God.

- An "epic" perspective on global events is being harnessed to get inside
what God is doing in the world — in this case bringing abundant life
even in the face of famine.

- A move is made to a lyric perspective — raising issues of hunger and
complex questions of eating disorders and perhaps even self-harm, together with more general concerns about being overweight and unat-
tractive. The key to this move lies in the two words *hunger* and *shame.*
Hunger is employed in a figurative way that makes a transition from the
explicit hunger in a famine to a more metaphorical hunger associated
with unresolved desire. Shame is a term that any pastor knows lingers
just under the surface of many, perhaps most, members of any congregation. Thus the prayer incorporates the distant needy, the distant
skilled, the nearby desperate, and the nearby concerned — all within a
handful of words and a sensitive tone of voice.

- A nod is made to the Eucharistic table as a sign of God's abundant
purpose expressed through food, and as a way of putting the world's

32

suffering in perspective. This is also a challenge to renew the sharing of food as a truly prayerful activity.

If a prayer can do all these things, no one will be concerned that it is short. Three or four petitions of this kind are plenty.

What is going on is not dissimilar to the prayerful practice known as *lectio divina*. In *lectio divina* an individual or group reads a scriptural passage once and meditates upon it; a second time and reflects upon words and contexts and resonance and meanings; a third time and synthesizes all the reflections and insights. In this style of petition the scriptural reference (in this case "your prophet Elijah came to the widow in a time of famine") becomes like the text, and there is a first level of reflection ("visit today the people of . . ."), which explores some of the byways of the information it dwells upon; then there is a second level of pondering ("work in the lives of all who work in the food service industry,") which stays with the notion of food and God's transformative action, but changes the setting to be more general ("incarnational"); then the mood remains incarnational and about God's ministry in food, but becomes more sharply pastoral, seeking subtly to name areas of pain and personal grief ("on all for whom food and body-image are a source of fear . . ."). Finally, the prayer moves to a mode of transfiguration, while staying with the same theme of food and God's action, and suggests the world as it might be if God answered the prayer ("Make us a people for whom food is a sign of your faithfulness . . .").

What exactly might it mean for God to answer this prayer?

Thus the members of the congregation are invited to see the connections between their own lives and the needs of people far away, between their own personal struggles and issues in public life, between the worship of their local community and the global questions that affect everyone; and they not only perceive but also genuinely feel a sense of the way God works in crisis, through people, and among those gathered to worship.

EXPECTING RESULTS

If a person is set aside to lead prayers for a community or a congregation, one question it is reasonable to expect her to have thought through during her time of preparation is, "What exactly might it mean for God to answer this prayer?" A prayer that says simply, "We pray for the Middle East, we remember those in China, we think of all the people of Haiti . . ." doesn't evidently address this question. As a consequence it may feel perfunctory and may express relatively little of the depth or challenge of the Christian faith.

Intercession remains a shadow of what it can be if the question of results is not addressed. Most people have experienced the confusion and ill-feeling that occurs when a friend or family member or employer or employee has only a general idea of what they expect of their counterpart, but, on finding their expectations unmet, becomes cross or troubled or hurt; quite often the real problem was that they never made their desires known, and simply assumed the other person would guess what they wanted or needed. Now, we are told that God knows what we need better than we do and anticipates our prayers before we ever make them; but that's no reason not to be specific in intercession. Being specific narrows down a general sense of unease into a particular request to act, and replaces a vague sense of God being distant with a focused and urgent desire for God to be present.

The world of business has developed a simple mnemonic for addressing such issues in the workplace. Targets should be SMART: specific, measurable, attainable, relevant, and time-sensitive. While God isn't an employee subject to key performance indicators, this language may be helpful for dispelling the vagueness to which public prayer is prone.

- *Specificity* encourages the intercessor not to say "the Middle East" but to focus on something much more concrete — at Christmas, for example, to focus on Bethlehem, or when considering the prophet Ezekiel to focus on Iraq, the contemporary location of the ancient Babylon.

- *Measurability* directs the prayer towards a sense of scale; just as news bulletins tend to focus on dramatic, violent incidents rather than abiding, chronic concerns, so intercessions often follow the action rather than looking for the underlying social issues. Matters for prayer are not by any means all about size, but if India and China comprise nearly half the world's population, it's not unreasonable to hope that their peoples will appear as subjects for intercession with some frequency.

- *Attainability* addresses vagueness in a different way. "Help all the people in the Middle East" is a prayer that expects God to care in a lot more detail than we do. It's not essential to grasp the differences between a Maronite Christian in Lebanon and a Melkite Christian in Israel, but to seek an attainable goal for both, it's appropriate to pray, "Give courage and strength to all Christians in Israel and its neighboring countries, and show them a future in which they can belong as Christians, as Arabs, and as citizens."

- *Relevance* is helpful particularly if a concern to be true to the shape of the scripture leads the intercessor to lose sight of the contemporary context. It's important to retain the sentiment of the scripture — but sometimes unhelpful to mimic its language too closely. Thus if the text for the day is Matthew 10:14-15 ("If anyone will not welcome you or listen to your words, shake off the dust from your feet as you leave that house or town. Truly I tell you, it will be more tolerable for the land of Sodom and Gomorrah on the day of judgment than for that town"), it's not necessarily conducive to invoke the story of Sodom and Gomorrah from Genesis 19; it may be better to say, "your Son Jesus encouraged us in mission and said that the fate of those who will not hear your voice is in your hands alone...."

- *Time-sensitivity* raises the question of the frequency of intercession. In 1 Thessalonians 5:17 Paul encourages Christians to pray without ceasing; and in Luke 18:1-8 Jesus commends the widow who relentlessly petitions the judge. There is something powerful in standing with one's foot in God's door and refusing to go away until the cry of the oppressed is heard. However, there is also much to be said for trusting the value of one single prayer, sincerely spoken, and not assuming more is better. Paying attention to anniversaries can be a way of combining these two goods.

In the business world, the SMART criteria are often associated with two other indicators, "evaluate" and "reevaluate" (hence SMARTER). The point is that such indicators don't work by themselves; they only do their work when closely monitored. Likewise in worship; if one really does expect God to answer intercessory prayer, it's important to create liturgical space to recognize and celebrate the answers God gives. A congregation (or a denomination) that has no such liturgical space is making a statement that it expects no such action on God's part. But that space is almost certainly not within the intercessions themselves, which are ruined if they turn into an evaluation and review process in which God is the employee. The ideal place is around the benediction, for, as we explored in chapter one, intercession is a plea that what I or others are currently going through may become a blessing, if not directly to us, then indirectly to others; and the blessing is an appropriate liturgical moment for counting and reflecting on such transformations.

BECOMING THE ANSWER TO PRAYER

In a conventional collect, the prayer begins with God (addressed by name), and then moves to God's action (as revealed in scripture), to the action sought today, to the desired result. That desired result is frequently focused on a change in the heart or mind of the intercessor or his or her community. For example, one standard Episcopal collect expresses the hope "that, when he comes again with power and great glory, we may be made like him in his eternal and glorious kingdom."[8] Likewise, in another Episcopal collect, the section expressing the desired result is as follows: "that with you as our ruler and guide we may so pass through things temporal that we lose not the things eternal." And again, this same collect continues: "that we, loving you in all things and above all things, may obtain your promises, which exceed all that we can desire."[9]

In a similar spirit, it has become common for Christians of the current era to adopt Gandhi's motto, "Be the change that you wish to see in the world." The sentiment is noble, and the words of the collects are beautiful, and there is much to be said for imitating both. The only danger is that the perfection of the self comes to be regarded — almost without question — as the point of prayer, the goal of a life's quest, and the ultimate purpose of God. Which it isn't.

A personal and pious climax to a petition is often moving, lyrical, and empowering and has many advantages, so long as three provisos are borne in mind. First, that this is not the invariable climax to the prayer — but instead is one of a variety of ways of concluding. Second, that this section is brief and does not take too much attention away from the primary focus, which should be the persons and places mentioned in the primary petition and the imperative verbs throughout. Third, that its attention is directed towards making the church a community of character and witness rather than making the individual fit for heaven.

8. *The Book of Common Prayer,* p. 236 (Proper 27).
9. *The Book of Common Prayer,* p. 231 (Proper 12).

If the intercessor adheres to these provisos, then a petition may helpfully end by looking with God to an outcome that sees the congregation, or the church more generally, as a great part of God's method of addressing the world's sadnesses and shortcomings. However, God has a purpose much broader than the redemption of the individual soul and much wider even than the sanctification of the church. Such hope is inspiringly identified in the Lutheran collect for the Ascension: "Almighty God, your only Son was taken into the heavens and in your presence intercedes for us. Receive us and our prayers for all the world, and in the end bring everything into your glory, through Jesus Christ, our Sovereign and Lord, who lives and reigns with you and the Holy Spirit, one God, now and forever."[10] Here is a larger purpose: the salvation, restoration, and redemption of all things.

And here we have arrived at the theological key to the whole shape of intercessory prayer. The problem is not, centrally, that people are suffering — although that grieves God's heart. Neither is the precise problem that people sin and bring tragedy upon others and themselves — miserable as that reality is. The whole purpose of creation and redemption is that all living things, through the collective priesthood of all believers, are called into the companionship of God and summoned to rejoice in God's presence forever. Intercession is an act of remembrance that this is God's purpose and remembrance of the way (in Christ) God embodies and goes about achieving that purpose; it is a naming of the symptoms and causes by which we can tell that that purpose is not yet wholly realized and a calling-upon God to realize it in those places; and it is a reorientation and renewal of the whole church toward the purpose it exists to serve.

Hence it is important that this climax of each petition echo, at least to some degree, the vision of the final purpose of God. For example, if the text for the day were the stilling of the storm; and the petition concerned survivors of a typhoon, or those losing their property and livelihood to rising flood waters acutely or chronically; and the subsidiary petition considered those facing metaphorical storms, of mental illness, a shaky economy, or fragile relationships; then the climax of the petition might say "that the earth may be filled with your glory as the waters cover the sea," or "that your righteousness may roll down like a never-failing stream." Such language locates scriptural witness and profound human need within the overarching purpose of God, which is to flood the earth with mercy and grace.

10. *Evangelical Lutheran Worship,* p. 35.

THREE

Social and Liturgical Context

THE PRAYERS OF THE PEOPLE are a moment where heart, hand, head, and gut all combine. The people's deepest cares, sifted through thoughtful and sensitive reflection, are put into plain and simple words. These prayers display the wide reach of the congregation's soul, the weight of the burdens these people carry together, the scope of this gathered body's concern for the worldwide church, and the compassion they share for local needs. The prayers can be a genuine lyric cry that names the struggles and doubts and longings of the ordinary Christian as well as an authentic articulation of the reality of life and faith in a marginal, fragile, or unusual context.

There are two main challenges about this aspect of intercessory prayer: how to ensure the congregation explicitly realizes what God is saying here, now, in this particular place and time; and how to ensure the congregation appreciates and enjoys that it is part of the body of Christ that worships in all times and places, now and forever. The issues of this chapter are about getting this balance right.

SOCIAL LOCATION

The most dangerous word in liturgy, especially informal, spontaneous liturgy, is "we." Those leading worship — especially any who are called to employ words that are not in the Bible or book of worship, for example by preaching a sermon, praying in any form, including a pastoral prayer, or making announcements — need to be vigilant about this slippery word. The word "we" is the most revealing word in intercessory prayer — but in ways that frequently undermine the aim of composing a pattern of petitions that every member of the congregation can say "Amen" to.

"We" means, on the surface, "I and people like me." But these people vary, and their number and identity may not be identical with the circumference of the communion of saints. Consider the following:

- Our troops
- Our country
- Our young people
- Our children's children
- Our environment

These are all common expressions, in the prayers of the people as elsewhere. The noun in question is not mysterious: everyone knows what troops, young people, and the environment are. But does the word "our" have a consistent meaning throughout? When an intercessor says in the midst of a congregation, "We pray for our country and our troops," where does that put any foreign nationals who happen to be present? They are not part of the "we." They have no doubt listened to an opening announcement about how welcome they are — but quickly they get a more subtle but perhaps more significant indication that they are not fundamentally part of the "we" of this community. Are they expected to say "Amen" at the end of this prayer? If so, the language of the prayer needs to change. What is being subtly stated is that there is a social grouping being assumed that requires something other than baptism or faith in the God of Jesus Christ. Nationality has become the governing criterion for belonging to this "we." Civil religion has displaced the church.

When it comes to "our young people," the "we" connotes something slightly different. The speaker almost certainly isn't referring to the children of his or her own nuclear family (to use "we" in such a narrow sense is obviously exclusive); this is more commonly a reference to the young people of the congregation. But again, where does this put a visitor to the congregation? A more subtle point is that those over seventy are often referred to as "older people" and those under twenty as "young people"; but those between twenty and seventy are not given an epithet: this gives an implicit message that church is really for them — because they are the norm. Meanwhile a term such as "our children's children" places those who don't themselves have children "outside" in a curious way: the phrase is usually employed in the context of concern about the world's future, but the quiet message here is that only those who have reared children have a direct investment in that future. The "we" has shifted again.

It's common to refer to "our world" or "our environment." But who is the "we" here? Surely part of the point of intercession is to recall that, as Paul insists, "The earth is the Lord's, and everything in it" (1 Cor. 10:25, quoting Psalm 24:1). The whole message of the ecological movement is to point out that there is more to the universe than that part that lies within each human person's own environs. These things are not "ours," however vague this "we" may in this case be. This instance provides the clue as to how to resolve the problem of the floating-yet-always-exclusive "we." The simple rule is to remember who is being addressed: God. If this is a conversation between the intercessor and God, "our" has to include God or not be used at all. Hence it's fitting to say "Your world"; but not to say "our children's children."

A further problem of the floating "we" is that it can turn compassion into subtle exclusion. "We pray for all who have HIV/AIDS, that they may find hope in their struggle, and friends in their isolation." Such a prayer makes it absolutely clear that, while having HIV/AIDS is a condition to evoke sympathy, it is something not experienced by "us"; it is something from which "they" suffer. It seems very unlikely, in this world-view, that someone could be a Christian and live with HIV. Similar language is often used for "the disabled" or "the homeless" — as if such people could not possibly be present and exist only as recipients of the congregation's pity and provision.

To avoid these pitfalls linguistically, avoid the words "we," "our," and "us" as much as possible, except perhaps in the climax of the prayer where the "we" explicitly means the worldwide church and does not inherently exclude anybody; avoid precise terminology that identifies social groupings by arbitrary characteristics; and refer instead more allusively to lyrical categories — "all for whom home is a place of danger," "any who know their appearance causes alarm to strangers," "those whose medical condition invites stigma and discrimination." But this is more of a problem of mind and heart than of language. Here is an example of how preparing prayers shapes moral perception — of how learning to speak about people in general may teach the intercessor how to relate to people in particular.

SINGING AND SPEAKING OF FAITH

The prayers of the people need to be true to their social place and time. But they can also be profoundly enriched by the ways they interact with their liturgical place and time. An act of worship is like a symphony, where each movement picks up and echoes and improvises upon the previous one,

Worship is like a symphony, where each movement picks up and echoes and improvises upon the previous one.

such that the whole is a reverberating sum of the different resonances of the parts. In the rest of this chapter we suggest ways to make that symphony sing through the intercessions.

Hymns and songs lie deep in the consciousness of many worshipers. If you're looking for something to do at the bedside of a struggling companion, perhaps the best thing of all is quietly to sing a suitable song or hymn into his or her ear. Hymns themselves are nothing other than sung prayers. So to quote a hymn — particularly if it is one of those selected for the day — is a way of helping the congregation pray twice. But because so many hymns and songs are so well known, odd lines can be quoted or rephrased in ways that both name and elucidate states of mind or heart.

Thus, if there has been an earthquake — or if there has been a figurative earthquake in the form of a notorious church dispute or divisive period in public life — the intercessor can simply conclude a petition, "Breathe through the earthquake, wind, and fire, O still small voice of calm," with every confidence that the congregation will recognize the words from the hymn "Dear Lord and Father of Mankind." Such a quotation not only deepens identification with the prayer but refreshes the worshipers' experience of the hymn. Likewise, if there has been a heavy loss of life in a battle or sudden disaster, a verse from "O God, Our Help in Ages Past" will be near the surface of the collective memory: "Time like an ever-rolling stream has rolled so many of your children away. . . ." Christmas carols are especially well-loved but not always so well pondered as they are sung; so incorporating stray lines in intercessory prayer renews both prayer and song: "Veiled in flesh you were pleased to dwell with us: be close to all who tonight find it hard to continue to dwell with members of their own household, or who are incarcerated with those with whom they cannot abide to dwell."

When a particular season — such as Easter or Advent — suggests itself, or when a particular occasion or tragedy arises, it may be suitable to base a whole prayer around a single well-known hymn or song. During Advent the verses of "O Come, O Come, Emmanuel" lend themselves to being formed into petitions; on Easter Day the verses of "Crown Him with Many Crowns" offer a shape for petitions that cover cross, resurrection, and ascension. After a maritime disaster it can be helpful to fold all prayers around the cadences of "Eternal Father, Strong to Save." Quoting hymns in this way is like two friends meeting for a coffee and citing previous happy or memorable times they have spent together: it enriches the current experience while refreshing the earlier ones. The congregation is not being pummeled with new information but is given the opportunity to enjoy old words with their new resonance. Like all such touches, it can be overdone, but it is an important dimension of the intercessor's repertoire.

> Quoting hymns is like two friends meeting for a coffee and citing previous happy or memorable times they have spent together.

The creed is a kind of hymn. It's usually spoken, rather than sung, and it's generally said solemnly, rather than with gusto: but it finishes with the word Amen, which turns it, like a hymn, into a kind of prayer. As with hymns, creeds can be renewed, and intercessions deepened in their resonance, by the introduction of familiar phrases in a different context. Thus "Maker of heaven and earth, for us and for our salvation you sent your only begotten Son Jesus as light from light: bring light to the people of . . ." Or alternatively "Lord and giver of life, you have spoken through the prophets; raise up prophets today in . . ." Or again, "Maker of all that is, seen and unseen, you teach us to look for the resurrection of the dead, and the life of the world to come; look with favor on your servant [name], who has died . . ." In such phrases are the different elements of the liturgy bound together, and the deep repertoire of the congregation is brought to fruition.

SERMON

We have already noted in chapter one that the prayers of the people are most definitely not an alternative sermon. But they can be enhanced — and the sermon greatly enriched — if they cover the same ground in different, but complementary ways.

It is ideal if the preacher's main themes — or perhaps even written words — can be communicated to the intercessor days before the service, and certainly before the intercessor prepares the petitions. If the petitions dovetail with the sermon, many possibilities are released. The sermon may be making three, related points: the prayers may take the same shape. The sermon may concentrate on one passage of scripture, largely ignoring any other passages that may have been read; the prayers may be able to incorporate those passages while keeping to the sermon's broad theme. The sermon may take a somewhat strident, "prophetic" tone, perhaps a little unforgiving and setting aside sensitivity for the sake of clarity and succinctness; the prayers may be able to cover the same ground in a gentler way, making gestures to those who fall outside the high standards and expectations of the preacher. The sermon may have a key phrase or text that's repeated for rhetorical or mnemonic effect; the prayers may echo that phrase or take it into new areas of significance. There may have been not one but two dramatic events in the news that week and the preacher can confidently explore one while knowing that the intercessor will suitably address the other.

This is what can happen when liturgy is planned and crafted by a cohesive and collaborative team, working in advance so as to look for serendipitous harmonies. The alternative can be as bad as the ideal is good. An intercessor can take the same passage as the preacher and treat it in an opposite or contradictory way, leaving the congregation confused. The intercessor may use a word positively that the preacher has criticized, or vice versa. The intercessor may completely ignore a contemporary issue that the preacher regarded as so important as to require becoming the focus of the whole sermon.

A well-organized preacher can transform the liturgy of even the most humble and understated congregation: a sermon whose theme, or perhaps full text, is available to colleagues and worship leaders several days before the service can set the tone for hymns, songs, an unusual but appropriate response to the sermon, words introducing confession, and a form of blessing, as well as suitable prayers. This is not a matter of extra "work," but simply better planning, higher aspirations, and clearer expectations from all parties. There is a correspondence between a clear, bold sermon that speaks *for* God, confident that God has something to say, and a straightforward, imperative time of prayer that speaks *to* God, confident that God is looking to act. A congregation has every reason to expect both.

ENRICHING WORSHIP

An intercessor who is well briefed (through being familiar with the contents of the sermon and the assigned music) and well prepared (having looked over the readings and been in touch with the local, national, and international news) can raise the level of a whole service. Thus a confession of sin can be simply "out of the book" with an introduction based on John 3:16 ("God so loved the world . . .") or Hebrews 4:14-16 ("Since we have a great high priest who has passed through the heavens, Jesus, the Son of God . . . Let us therefore approach the throne of grace with boldness, so that we may receive mercy and find grace . . ."); but it can be based, like the prayers of the people, around the readings. And if the person leading the prayers of the people and the person overseeing the confession of sin are able to plan and coordinate, then the prayers of the people can pick up the aspects of the day's theme that address suffering, while the confession can address that aspect that engages sin.

Here, for example, is a confession of sin arising from Jesus' call of the first disciples, blending themes of Epiphany and discipleship:

God in Christ calls us to follow, but we shy or run away. Yet God comes to
meet us and heal us, and holds out beckoning hands that we may walk
with the Holy Spirit forever. Let us confess our sins that we may rejoice in
God's company.
You want us to walk as children of light;
but we have hidden in the shadows.
Lord, have mercy, **Lord, have mercy.**
You want us to see your brightness;
but we have mistrusted and misrepresented you.
Christ, have mercy, **Christ, have mercy.**
You want us to look for your coming,
but we have put our hopes in lesser things.
Lord, have mercy, **Lord, have mercy.**

And here is the first petition in the prayers of the people for that same day:

Beckoning God, in Christ you have fished for us.
Be close to all, who, like James and John, work all night, and those who
make their living at sea.
Bless spouses and children and parents whose loved ones spend long
periods away on the ocean.
Encourage any who, like Zebedee, watch as their children are called to
ministry that takes them far from home to places of danger and fear.
Give us faith and courage to be like James and John, and follow you,

catching fish with you; but give us strength when we sense, like Zebedee,
that the real action in your kingdom is elsewhere.
Lord, in your mercy, **hear our prayer.**

Beyond the sermon, the hymns, and the confession of sin, the other part of the service with which the prayers of the people really should connect is the announcements. What are the announcements, if not items for the congregation's prayer and action in the week to come and beyond? Announcements are the part of the service that are habitually given the least preparation but perhaps cause the most offense — because of what is included, a disparaging tone in which some things are described, or the way some things seem never to be included. The announcements are an anomaly in worship — because they are an extended period which is neither about God talking to the people nor about the people talking to God; they are about helping people talk to each other, although often in a rather elongated way. But if the announcements and the prayers of the people are describing entirely different things, there is some kind of a problem: either the prayers of the people have lost touch with the daily life and concerns of the congregation, or the announcements have lost touch with the fact that this is a community gathered to worship God.

If all is well, then there should be a good deal of overlap between the two. If a couple is getting married, and such an event is mentioned in the announcements, then a reference in the prayers of the people fits well. If a summer fair is approaching, and volunteers are to be rallied in the announcements, then the central purpose of the fair should surely feature in the prayers of the people too. As with the sermon, so with the announcements: the prayers of the people may pick up a different side to the same issue, perhaps highlighting those who are not party to the celebrations in question — for example remembering those who would like to be married but are not, or any who have found marriage to be more of a burden than a blessing.

There are particular occasions when, if a layperson is leading the prayers of the people, while the pastoral leader of the community is giving the announcements, the announcements may be a place for a brief extra intercession. If there is a great event in the community or beyond — particularly if that event may be in some way hidden from the congregation, but nonetheless not unduly personal — the pastor may judge it helpful to conclude the announcements with a direct and uncomplicated plea. For example, if there has been a painful death leaving a devastating bereavement, or an accident leaving a person clinging to life, or the nation stands on the brink of war, or the judicatories of the church are about to vote on a matter close to the church's identity and core mission, then the pastoral leader may judge this is a moment for a petition outside the normal way of things, and call the congregation to a spontaneous prayer. Such moments can be powerful and memorable, but only if they are rare.

Two other factors, beyond the scriptural themes and the news of the day, should affect the content of the prayers of the people: cycles of prayer and the liturgical year. Anyone who intercedes daily knows that there's just too much to keep in your head. It's not just the "resurrection" prayers for those in crisis; it's the "incarnation" prayers for all whom you long to be close to God's heart. So there's no avoiding a list. Some traditions do this through annual cycles of prayer that cover praying for elected leaders at local, state, and national levels, or for every street in one's neighborhood, or for every county or suburb in a major metropolitan area, or for each nation of the world. A list ensures that, while one can't pray for everyone every day, one can pray for everyone over a period of time. The same is true of the liturgical year: there are times for celebration (Easter), penitence (Lent), and remembrance (All Saints), and many more. There are also more specific seasons — the week of prayer for Christian unity, World Communion Sunday, and so on.

A congregation that commits itself to honor such cycles and seasons in its prayers is simply being humble and recognizing how easy it would otherwise be to forget, overlook, or neglect subjects and locations that don't readily come to mind. But it is not necessary — indeed, it is wearisome — to draw attention to such patterns of intercession: phrases such as "in our cycle of prayer, we remember . . . ," or "at this season we call to mind . . ." are deadly, not least because they are addressed to the congregation and not to God. (Such things can be done in a newsletter, if necessary.) The secret is to weave the cyclical and annual subjects into the prayers just as one does with the scriptural themes and topical information. If two or more subjects blend into one another — if praying for the church in Cape Town becomes a prayer for Southern Africa as a whole — so much the better.

THE OFFERING

Prayer is not simply a verbal thing. Liturgy is an enacted prayer. The sitting and standing, the movement of hands in blessing, the architecture of the building, the touch and eye-contact of sharing peace, the music, the liturgical colors, the texture of vessel and cloth, the breaking of bread: all of these shape the prayer.

Where it is a regular feature of worship, the offertory procession is a tradition that can be built upon. The procession most often includes monetary gifts, and, if a Eucharist is to follow, Communion elements of bread and wine. The bread may be taken to represent ordinary human endeavor; the wine may be taken to represent extraordinary human longing; together they synthesize God's work and ours. Meanwhile the money is a token of our giving back to God everything that God has first given us. There is much here to savor and ponder: it's a visual prayer of dedication and thanksgiving, of service and hope, of faithfulness and expectation. It's the moment when the summation of the human story is presented to God for transformation by God's story.

This is a rich tradition. But it's one that can be inhabited further. The prayers of the people can become part of the offering. Just as an offertory procession is a way of saying to God, "This is the best we can do; now you must take over," so intercessions are saying, "We have nothing more to give; we need you to do the rest." This can be moving and helpful if done in tangible form. Here are three ways in which intercessory word can be made flesh.

1. Suppose a local young man had died suddenly, perhaps by suicide, and the family had asked to hold the funeral at your church. Suppose the young man had been pursuing medical research in the course of doctoral studies. Suppose there were people in his life who'd been trying for some time to be closer to him, to give him support and strength in his many struggles. Might it be a beautiful gesture, in the face of their grief and sense of powerlessness, to invite two or three of them, during the offertory procession the next Sunday, to bring forward the young man's lab coat and some of his research implements, to say in the poetry of movements what it is hard to put into words?

2. Suppose the church was set in the midst of many shops, government buildings, schools, and businesses, and suppose there was a question of how best to relate to these centers of activity. Suppose a cycle of prayer was drawn up by which it was planned to pray for each of these organizations on one Sunday of the year, respectively. A letter could be written, perhaps hand-delivered, which asked if there were particular

items for which the leader or members of the organization would appreciate prayer (or for which they might wish publicly to give thanks), and which invited the organization to send someone to carry a suitable symbol forward in the offertory procession on the assigned Sunday?

3. Suppose a great tragedy had taken place in which someone had massacred a number of people, or an accident had taken the lives of many passers-by. Suppose a line of people, equal to the number deceased, and perhaps of corresponding age or station in life, were asked each to bring forward a rose of an appropriate color and lay it on or beneath the altar during the offertory procession, remembering the dead and the bereaved in the context of recalling Jesus' life laid down so that all might live abundantly. Would that not be more touching, more empowering, than a traditional minute of silence or a simple prayer for all involved?

These are all ways in which, through planning and care, worship can come to mean a great deal not just to the regular congregation, but also to those who may be unfamiliar with the hope that is in the congregation's heart and yet have so much to give to and gain from the church. Intercession is perhaps the most basic and visceral prayer of all — "O God, help me." The church should be able to turn that most common and desperate of prayers into a form of life which gives purpose to and derives meaning from the rest of its life and worship.

FOUR

Shaping the People

ASK. SEEK. KNOCK. JESUS DESCRIBED prayer in all three of these dimensions. "Ask, and it will be given to you; seek, and you will find; knock, and the door will be opened for you" (Matt 7:7). Asking is verbal; it draws upon words. The preceding chapters have explored how to ask. This chapter is about seeking and knocking. Seeking and knocking are not so much verbal as physical and incarnational. Seeking involves head and heart, eyes and hands, smell and taste; it is a disposition of eager attention. It is the disposition of the sniffing dog, the retriever. Knocking requires the body. It is kinesthetic; the very movement itself conveys belief and hope and expectation, in a context of respectful but hopeful waiting. To ask, to seek, and to knock, in concert with others, is the essence of congregational intercessory prayer. This chapter is about how worship shapes our seeking and knocking; it is about how we inhabit these embodied dimensions of prayer together as a community of faith.

LET US PRAY

In many churches, the person leading intercession invites the congregation to a time of prayer with the exchange of these words:

The Lord be with you.
And also with you.
Let us pray.

It is an invitation of inclusion, signaling that what follows is a corporate act. The energies and concentration of all present, from the oldest to the youngest, from the week-by-week faithful to the first-time visitor, are needed to enact together the liturgy of prayer.

The intercessor says not, "Let *me* pray," but rather, "Let *us* pray." While the intercessor's role is speaking to God for the people, prayer in public worship is not something the intercessor does apart from the people. It is fundamentally something the intercessor does *with* the community of those gathered. The invitation, "Let *us* pray," presumes that the people have a role to play as well. That the intercessor is speaking to God on the people's behalf is the first part to make clear; but when that part is well defined, God's people are set free to enter the conversation between Father, Son, and Holy Spirit. They are welcomed into the prayer of the church around the world and throughout time.

> God's people are set free to enter the conversation between Father, Son, and Holy Spirit.

The words of intercession may be crafted ever so carefully, the nuance may be profound, the balance of local, national, and international attention may be perfect. Even so, the people of God gathered to worship are not distantly prayed *for* by the intercessor. Prayers of intercession are often called Prayers of the People. Notably, they are not called Prayers *for* the People; they are called Prayers *of* the People. Though the intercessor is the one responsible for speaking, the liturgy of prayer comes alive as it is embodied by the whole congregation. Precisely how the people of God are made ready for this duty and joy is a matter that beckons our imagination.

SHAPING THE PEOPLE FOR PRAYER

Thus far we have focused on shaping the words for prayer in public worship. Now we are ready to consider the second aspect: shaping the people to pray. Shaping the words and shaping the people are intertwined. Shaping the people to pray means attending to the embodied, environmental dimensions of the worship space. Everything about the physical setting for worship, the location of the intercessor within the worship space, and the bodily positions of both intercessor and congregation communicate an understanding of what we believe is happening when we pray. Shaping the people to pray means inviting the people to participate in visible, tangible ways which communicate what we believe prayer really is.

In American mainline churches, a rich diversity has emerged through a variety of traditional, contemporary, blended, and emergent worship services. Each presents a unique setting for congregational intercessory prayer. Even within the same church, a pastor may find herself offering prayer in a variety of worship settings. Perhaps there is a small chapel for an early morning service, a fellowship hall for a contemporary service, a sanctuary for a traditional service, and a congregant's home for an emergent evening service. While the style appropriate for each of these settings will, and should, vary, we will now explore how the imagination of the congregation can best be shaped through the way the prayer is embodied by the congregation and the intercessor.

EMBODIED THEOLOGICAL ASPIRATIONS

Whether worship takes place in a traditional setting where practices of prayer are highly ritualized, or in a new worship space where practices of prayer are shaped purposely in less conventional ways, the prayers of the people are embodied by the intercessor and congregation together. While it is good to be creative, it is also wise to have a theological framework to shape our aspirations for prayer. In other words, the setting may vary, but the liturgical purpose and theological basis of such prayer remains the same. The purpose of this chapter is to draw our attention to the most significant theological elements of the prayers of the people and to imagine how they can best be put into practice.

These are the most significant theological aspirations for the prayers of the people:

1. The prayer is directed to God through every element of word, gesture, bodily posture, and physical space.

2. The people adopt a posture which trusts the intercessor and believes God will draw near.

3. The intercessor carries the people's deepest needs to God, thereby drawing the people more closely into God's presence.

Let's now explore each of these aspirations in detail.

THE PRAYER IS DIRECTED TO GOD

We have already discussed in detail how the words of the prayer should be directed to God, rather than about God. Every element of the worship environment can contribute to orienting the congregation for this moment of speaking to God. The most important thing is not to miss any opportunity to orient the congregation toward God for the time of prayer.

The posture and placement of the intercessor immediately direct the congregation's attention. Precisely where the intercessor physically occupies space communicates a significant nonverbal message. One of the most confusing things an intercessor can do is to pray from a location in the worship space that is not meant for speaking to God. In a traditional sanctuary, the lectern and pulpit are prime examples of areas that are meant for speaking on God's behalf to the people. When they are used for speaking on the people's behalf to God it sends a confusing message to the congregation. It is much better to offer the prayers of the people from elsewhere.

Where is that "elsewhere"? Areas that are used for speaking to God include the altar or communion table, and in some churches, the chancel rail. In some traditions the intercessor takes up a position in the aisle, perhaps two-thirds of the way towards the back, facing in the same direction as the congregation, to affirm solidarity with them and to demonstrate that the prayers are coming from the heart of the congregation. These areas are best suited for leading prayer in a sanctuary setting. In less conventional worship spaces, those leading worship must give careful thought to which areas are used for speaking to God and which are used for speaking to the people. For example, perhaps a lectern used for the sermon is moved aside during the prayer to allow the intercessor to come physically closer to the congregation. This shift makes clear that the time of speaking to the people for God is finished and the time of speaking to God for the people has come. Perhaps everything on the stage is removed entirely for the time of prayer to direct a singular focus on God. Or perhaps the person leading prayers comes down from a stage onto the floor where the people are seated to signal a more intimate time with God.

Worshipers can also be visually oriented by carefully chosen projected images. Simple pictures such as hands folded together or candles burning can offer a focal point. Alternatively, if visual projection is used during other parts of worship, darkening the screen entirely for prayer can help direct focus toward God. Lighting overall, especially dimmed lights, which are often common in less conventional settings, can further foster a sense of focus. Perhaps there is a focal point, like lit candles, which have been burning all along but become more visible once lights are low.

After attending to the physical space, then physical posture, particularly the posture of the intercessor, becomes important. In any setting, the posture of the intercessor has the potential to direct the people toward God or distract them from such focus. The intercessor either kneels or stands. A kneeling intercessor visually focuses the congregation's attention on coming before God in holiness, humility, and human need. A kneeling intercessor displays her consciousness of being on holy ground, in the presence of the living God. Kneeling is a posture that assumes the words to come are weighty and spoken with careful consideration. Even more so, kneeling communicates that the person on her knees has the patience to await a response, for she has entered into divine conversation. A standing intercessor visually centers the congregation's attention on coming before God in the confidence and boldness of the Holy Spirit.

The posture of the intercessor communicates the spirit in which the congregation together approaches God's throne of grace.

Throughout the history of the church, standing at particular points of the liturgy is taken to represent resurrection hope. Thus, a standing intercessor physically proclaims resurrection in the midst of the cares and concerns of human life. Whatever trials and troubles are spoken in the petitions, the promise of God's redeeming work stands over all. Both understandings of prayer are rich in what they say about God, so it is worth considering which communicates the message appropriate to the gathered congregation and, given all the elements of the worship environment, which best directs the congregation to God.

Sometimes the posture of the intercessor is obscured because of fumbling with a bulletin or notes, or the script of the prayer, or a microphone, or whatever else might be in hand. When the intercessor himself is distracted by these fumbles, it's safe to assume the congregation is distracted too. Clearly if one follows the recommendations here to write prayers ahead of time in preparation for worship, there will be a piece of paper to carry in hand. It can always be tucked inside a bulletin or hymnal, without drawing undue attention. What's important is that the congregation is aware of the posture and presence of the intercessor more than they are aware of whatever is carried in hand. The posture of the intercessor communicates the spirit in which the congregation together approaches God's throne of grace.

Imagine you are out walking in the forest with a friend, and after a while you come to an open field with a scenic view and want to sit down there for a while. How would you communicate with your friend? You would pause your footsteps, make eye contact with one another, and acknowledge verbally that yes, this is a good place. Then you might sit together for a good long while, taking in the view. Think about what happens in such a simple interaction. Fundamentally you pause, you make eye contact with one another, exchange a few words, and then you divert your eyes together to yet another view. The invitation to prayer beckons the kind of shared focus that comes through directing our attention together in a particular way.

The very first thing the intercessor does in directing the people toward God is to invite them to pray. It generally happens very quickly, but it's absolutely essential. In some settings this invitation comes in a formal way: "The Lord be with you. **And also with you.** Let us pray." In other settings, it comes in a conversational tone: "Would you pray with me?" Either way, the invitation to pray is like making eye contact with someone, which establishes a vital human connection, and then together looking to God in prayer. This invitation is part of the way the intercessor draws the congregation into the presence of God, which we'll address in greater detail later. For now, it's crucial to establish the role of the intercessor in inviting the congregation to pray. It would be a mistake for the intercessor to assume that the words of invitation to prayer are rote liturgy, even when the same invitation is used every week. It would be a greater mistake for the intercessor simply to begin praying by speaking to God without inviting the congregation to join. The words must be truly, sincerely issued as an invitation to play their part in welcoming the congregation into the Trinitarian conversation. It's the subtle difference between saying to a friend, "Sure, come for dinner if you like" and "I'd be so delighted if you came to my house for dinner tonight. Please do come." The latter communicates the deep pleasure and joy anticipated by having the company of another person. The invitation to prayer should communicate this kind of sincerity.

The intercessor's consciousness of every element of word, gesture, bodily posture, and physical space coalesce as he moves into the space for prayer, assumes a particular position, and speaks an invitation. All of these elements converge to play their part in directing the prayerful focus of the congregation to God.

THE PEOPLE TRUST THE INTERCESSOR AND BELIEVE GOD WILL DRAW NEAR

Just as the participation of the people in prayer can be too easily overlooked, so too can the posture of the people. While God is obviously not unduly concerned with the people's posture and it is secondary to God's hearing of the people's cries, the posture of the people says everything about their expectations of what will happen during this sacred time. Let's consider a very conventional approach to prayer where the members of the congregation bow their heads and close their eyes. Closing one's eyes is fundamentally an expression of trust. It communicates trust in someone else, and it communicates a willingness to be led somewhere sight unseen. When an intercessor begins prayer in the midst of a room full of people with eyes closed, he must realize he's been given a tremendous trust. The people are trusting him with their souls before God. Similarly, a bowed head signals a readiness for God to draw near. To bow our heads and close our eyes in prayer embodies our belief that, in drawing near, God comes in pure goodness and grace. We need not be on guard, only ready to receive. It is important that the people's participation in prayer communicates this expectant hope in God's goodness toward us.

In some denominations, the people are invited to change posture for prayer. They may be invited to stand or to kneel. As we described earlier, standing and kneeling each embody hope. Standing represents resurrection hope while kneeling represents the hope of coming onto holy ground in the presence of the living God. Standing or kneeling also offers an embodied way to differentiate the time of prayer from what has happened before and what will follow in the worship service. When the people change position, they direct their physical focus toward God. This change of posture is a way of becoming ready for God to draw near, preparing expectantly in hope. It also communicates their trust in the leadership of the person leading prayers and in the places that person will take them in prayer. It signals their ready participation in what is to come.

Of course there are other postures for prayer, but most important is that it is a posture of expectation and trust. In blended, contemporary, and emergent services, there are abundant opportunities for the people to embody different postures of prayer. Perhaps worshipers are invited to look at their own two open hands or to focus on their neighbor's hands during the time of intercession. The petitions could be based around how hands are used in everyday ways, and explore how hands can offer mercy, gentleness, and strength in time of need. Or perhaps each person is given a simple object to hold to orient her prayer. For example, if the focus for the day is the parable of the pearl of great price, each worshiper could be given a pearl to hold. The petitions could be based on themes of discovering that God holds each of us as the pearl of great price, and he has sold everything to call us his own. Forms of prayer which consciously involve the body help us become more aware of what we hope happens when we pray, especially when we become involved in ways that embody what we believe. This, of course, is the calling of every disciple — to become what we profess.

The intercessor plays a role in defining the space, time, and activity appropriate to congregational participation in prayer. Many churches have prayer cards in the pew racks, which offer worshipers a way to name particular requests. Prayer stations are also increasingly common in emergent and contemporary settings. At the prayer station there might be candles and prayer cards for naming particular requests. Sometimes prayer stations may have only objects, intended to evoke certain forms of prayer. There may be symbolic items to hold, like a broken plate at a station oriented toward prayer for broken places in our lives, the church, and the world. There may also be a person (perhaps a congregation member) available nearby to pray with anyone who comes, if desired. It's important to define when these additional avenues of prayer are open to the congregation and to extend a clear invitation, even though participation is optional.

What's important about the people's participation is that they become ready for God to draw near. Yes, the intercessor hopes they will join an assenting "Amen" at the end to all that has been said; but moreover, the intercessor seeks to ensure that all she has done to direct attention and invite embodied participation draws out the people's deepest yearning to encounter the living God.

THE INTERCESSOR CARRIES THE
PEOPLE'S DEEPEST NEEDS TO GOD

The intercessor inhabits a holy place where two praying hands meet. One hand represents God drawing near to the people, and the other hand represents the people drawing near to God. Imagine two hands coming together, palms facing each other, but touching only at the fingertips. The intercessor occupies the small space in between and embodies a fervent hope that indeed God and the people will draw near to one another.

Drawing the people more closely into God's presence isn't something that can be done *for* others; but it is something that can be invited and encouraged. Some may be intimidated by prayer, so it is the role of the intercessor to create a framework within which an encounter with God can happen. While ultimately grace alone allows us to draw near to God, the intercessor embodies this hope in a number of ways.

> The intercessor inhabits a holy place where two praying hands meet. One hand represents God drawing near to the people, and the other hand represents the people drawing near to God.

In some congregations, as we have noted, the intercessor is physically present in the midst of the people. The intercessor may stand in the midst of the assembled congregation, especially if the seating is arranged in a circle or semicircle or if there is a central aisle. This is particularly effective if the intercessor faces in the same direction as the people and speaks from among them rather than to them. In this arrangement, the intercessor is physically very close to the people, which is the embodiment of knowing, understanding, and carrying the needs of the people into God's presence.

Another possibility is for the intercessor to come to a lower chancel rail, on the level where the congregation is seated, and to kneel to lead the prayer from the chancel rail. In this posture, the person leading prayers symbolically kneels in God's presence on behalf of the congregation, as one of them. Having someone go ahead of them to begin the conversation with God can be an inspiration to those who have come with cares and concerns on their hearts but don't know where to begin when it comes to laying those bare before God. Microphones make such an interplay of intimacy and distance possible.

Both of these postures communicate a sense of intimacy between the intercessor and the congregation, by both physical proximity and common identification. And that names the key thing an intercessor can do to help the people draw near to God: foster a sense of intimacy.

In some settings, the person leading prayers is physically more distant from the people. For example, the intercessor may lead from a high altar or communion table. When a sense of intimacy is lacking in this situation, it is especially noticeable because there is less physical proximity to help. The sense that the intercessor has gone to God on their behalf — but without bringing them along — can deflate the whole experience of prayer. When the prayers of the people are led from a high altar or communion table, the person leading prayers carries the needs of the congregation, the church, and the world in a distinct way. More than any other time, carefully crafted petitions that convey the breadth and depth of need show the congregation that the intercessor indeed knows their hearts. In this situation, a moment of silence toward the end of the petitions is a particularly effective way to make room for each person's most urgent prayer to find a home in the heart of God. Warmth and strength of body language, along with care for spoken language, help the congregation with the sense that the intercessor has drawn near to them and invites them to draw near to God.

The sense of intimacy in prayer is by no means precluded by any setting, even in very large spaces. It does require consideration of the worship space, though, and an awareness of the extent to which the space can deepen prayer or distract from it. What's key is to realize it doesn't have to be small to be intimate in a way that draws people to God; neither does smallness guarantee the kind of intimacy required for prayer. The physical proximity of the intercessor is also no guarantee that the person leading fosters the kind of intimacy that allows the people to draw near to God. Intimacy can be an elusive aspect of congregational prayer. When it's neglected, it's because the person leading assumes it's not needed or required or simply isn't sure how to foster that sense in worship or isn't comfortable displaying that dimension in prayer. But if the intercessor can't display some way of drawing near to the people, it's very hard indeed for the people to trust that this person can help them draw near to God.

In cases where the intercessions fall within the Pastoral Prayer, the same considerations should be given to each of the areas explored here: the physical environment, the posture and placement of the praying pastor within it, and any expectations for congregational participation. The theological aspirations named in this chapter are equally suitable for guidance in shaping a Pastoral Prayer. When intercessions are but a single component of a more comprehensive prayer, one challenge can be to differentiate the time of prayer from other moments when the pastor is leading worship. Pastors easily fall into the habit of using the same lectern or pulpit for most of their speaking. If a microphone that allows movement is an option, then other locations, as have been mentioned here, become readily available: the chancel rail, the communion table, an aisle in the midst of the congregation. Likewise, positions other than standing become possible;

but whatever placement and posture are chosen should be theologically suitable for the prayer as a whole. There is also some work to be done to make clear the role of the congregation in the time of prayer as the pastor embraces the expectation of praying on their behalf; particularly as there may be fewer embodied, verbal, or responsive ways for the congregation to join in.

CREATING A COMMUNITY OF PRAYER

The rhythm of weekly intercession aims to create a community of prayer. A community of prayer lives shared ways of speaking and shared ways of listening in the presence of God. While in some congregations, the same person may invariably be responsible for leading the prayers of the people, in many settings the intercessor will be a different person each week. Depending upon the size and flavor of the congregation, the intercessor may be a layperson or a clergyperson. There may be a team of laypeople, all gifted in prayer, who rotate leadership among themselves. Likewise, there may be multiple clergy on a staff who take turns to lead prayer.

There are two sets of challenges to creating a community of prayer: continuity and diversity. The challenge when prayers are led by a rotating team is continuity. Continuity is not uniformity. There will, and should be, a natural variety of expression introduced by having different people write and lead prayers each week. The challenge of continuity is about structuring the prayers of the people so that they become part of a sustained conversation from week to week. One of the most direct ways of fostering continuity in the prayers offered in worship is having regular conversation among those who lead prayer. When laity are the primary intercessors, gathering together with one another and the priest or pastor for reflection on the content, shape, and style of prayers can be most helpful. Likewise, if the prayers are led by a rotating team of clergy, regular reflection with one another can shape the range of concerns and the aspirations for the prayers of the people within a particular congregation. Deepening the sense of community among those who lead prayer is essential to cultivating week-to-week continuity. Discussing how to pray about topics that are sensitive or matters that are difficult for the particular congregation can enrich the prayers greatly. If the time for prayer includes inviting the

> The rhythm of weekly intercession aims to create a community of prayer.

congregation to share their concerns aloud, then there may be fruitful reflection about how best to facilitate this sharing and about the range of particular concerns that tend to arise during this time in the worship service. The first step towards creating a community of prayer within a congregation as a whole is cultivating a shared understanding among those who regularly lead this part of the liturgy.

If the same layperson or clergyperson leads the prayers of the people each week, then it is achieving diversity of expression, style, and range of concerns that requires special attention. The challenge for the solo intercessor is not to get stuck. Here is where the themes presented in scripture, music, and sermon offer fresh material each week with which to bring to God the concerns of the church, local community, and the world. If members of the congregation have the opportunity to name concerns on prayer cards, those offer the solo intercessor a window into the heart of the congregation and inform the shaping of prayers indirectly, even if particular concerns aren't to be named publicly.

Sustaining prayer as a week-to-week conversation requires sufficient continuity that a congregation comes to inhabit particular ways of speaking, and listening, and being together in the presence of God; and it requires sufficient diversity to make clear that we have cares and hopes to bring to God this Sunday that we did not have last Sunday: particular things have happened in the world, in our lives, in the church, and we can't begin to know what they mean until we consciously name them in God's redeeming presence. Sustaining a week-to-week conversation with diversity and continuity shapes the people to pray in ways that are in communion with one another in the same congregation and, at the same time, in communion with the great company of saints on earth and in heaven. It's important that the person leading prayers understands that what she is really doing is bringing the people into a conversation that is already going on, an everlasting conversation which beckons the community of prayer on earth to become one with the community of prayer in heaven.

The intercessor's role is to ask, trusting she will be given; to seek, trusting she will find; and to knock, trusting heaven's door will indeed be opened. It is not that she finds it easier to approach or talk to God than anyone else. Her job is simply to seek the threshold of heaven, to knock, and to enter with faith into the space where saints and angels pray without ceasing.

FIVE

Fine Tuning

ET'S SUPPOSE YOU HAVE AN understanding of what intercessory prayer is and of how theologians have taken it to work in the heart of God. Let's imagine that you have a sense of the shape of liturgy, of the difference between speaking to God and speaking for God, of the respective values and roles of confession, sermon, creed, thanksgiving, and announcements. Let's think that you appreciate both the epic external movements of history and the lyric internal reasons of the heart. Let's hope that you have a grasp of the form of a collect, of its five elements — addressing God, invoking a scriptural precedent, calling on God to act, imagining an outcome, and concluding. Let's take it that you've gained a reasonable perception of the scriptures assigned for the day and the matters in the local, national, and international news that suggest themselves for intercession at this time. Let's say that you and your congregation have thought through the significance of gesture, posture, physical location, and movement. Let's also assume, a stretch as it may be in some cases, that there is some kind of communication system either in practice or at least possible between those invited to lead prayers and those asked to preach and lead the rest of the service, particularly the confession of sin and the announcements.

This chapter supposes all those things and looks at ways to enhance or adjust the prayers of the people so that they become all that they can be for the glory of God and for the up-building of the church in the light of God's coming kingdom.

REPETITION

Repetition can be galvanizing and reassuring; it can also be dull and careless. Let's look at repetition in a macro and a micro sense.

There is a place for repetition of whole sections of prayer, but it's a small one. Those used to formal prayers delivered largely straight from a denominational prayer book may have grown up with resonant collects strung together and interspersed with generally rudimentary topicality:

> *Guide the people of this land, and of all the nations, in the ways of justice and peace; that we may honor one another and serve the common good . . .*

> *Bless all whose lives are closely linked with ours, and grant that we may serve Christ in them, and love one another as he loves us.*[1]

Such prayers remain lodged in the memory from hundreds of repetitions, and they meet most of the criteria set out in chapter two above — with imperative verbs and an idea of what an answer to the prayer might look like (although the appearance of the dangerous word "may" in both petitions indicates a drift toward a sermonic speaking to the congregation rather than an intercessory speaking to God). Prayers in this form certainly instill a simple structure and checklist — of addressing first church, then world, then ourselves, then the sick, then the dead.

In one congregation the person who usually offered intercessions at the midweek service was unexpectedly absent one afternoon. The pastor looked around the room, silently acknowledging with the small congregation that there was a hiatus in proceedings. He didn't want to presume anyone would step forward, nor did he want to simply carry on himself, without quickly checking to see if anyone else felt a call to lead prayers that day. "I'll do it," said a quiet voice — the voice of a woman who couldn't read or write, who'd had very little education, who'd not grown up in any kind of regular household, who often mistook her vocabulary, and who was used to being overlooked. "I'll do it," she said, as she shuffled forward in her round-shouldered way. Her prayers were matter-of-fact, direct, and followed a perceptible course through church and world and local community needs. They were admirably brief. The pastor didn't imagine she had ever raised her voice in public before: but here she was leading the people

---

1. *The Book of Common Prayer* (New York: Church Publishing Corp., 1979), p. 388.

of God in priestly prayer. It was everything the rhythm of repetition could ever hope to produce: it was beautiful and good and true.

But what a missed opportunity the prayers of the people can often be. Here is a moment of spontaneity, of color and life and variation and topicality and genuine structuring of new words around deepest convictions. Prayer for themselves and others is possibly the biggest single thing that draws people to a service of worship. And yet how frequently are such people met with lifeless, formulaic, turgid, predictable mantras? Of course the prayers should not be so wacky and original that they distract from the simple task in hand. But those prayers need to be both epic and lyric — to capture the outside world as it is but also the inner world as it feels. They need to speak of timeless realities but also to name immediate concerns.

So a balance of the new and the familiar is best. For example, there's nothing wrong with always sticking to three or four petitions. It's well worth having a checklist such as "church, world, ourselves, the sick, the dead," and better still to have a healthy balance between issues of (1) global, (2) national, and (3) local significance with the (4) wider church and the (5) congregation corporately and (6) individually — not as an agenda to be trotted through, but as a guide to ensure nothing important has been left out. But the routine should always be more or less invisible amid the more compelling dimension of the specially-crafted, the carefully-chosen, and the thoughtfully-ordered.

> **Prayers need to be both epic and lyric — to capture the outside world as it is but also the inner world as it feels.**

Moving from macro to micro, there is a place for repetition in the prayers of the people, in the sense that intercession is a form, albeit a specialized one, of public rhetoric. Consider a petition such as this:

God of mercy and grace,
your prophet Isaiah prayed that the heavens drop down from above
*   and the skies pour forth righteousness;*
drop down from heaven today upon the people of Y in their suffering;
drop down upon all who have lost loved ones, and search in vain for breath,
*   for possessions, for hope;*
drop down upon all who seek to lead the people in their bewilderment, to
*   restore order, to bring relief, to safeguard public health;*
drop down upon all who strive to bring expertise and assistance from
*   overseas....*

65

Here the repetition is compelling and draws the congregation into a spiral of concern and compassion, where each layer amplifies the foregoing one and takes the prayer deeper into the heart of God.

However, repetition in a casual way is distracting and sometimes irritating, since it indicates the intercessor hasn't reflected carefully on the words used and the nuances of different concerns, settling instead for a catch-all phrase. Certain kinds of words it is hard to avoid repeating. "We pray for . . ." can be difficult to avoid, but once it's been acknowledged that any use of "we" in a public prayer is problematic, that such a phrase draws more attention to those praying than to God who is being addressed, and that such a sentence structure takes attention away from the imperative verb that indicates what God is being asked to do, then this language may best be edited out altogether.

Second, and more subtly, when making lists, especially in subordinate petitions, it can be easy to fall into repeating "those who" several times. There are alternatives: "any," "all," and "the many" can be useful; but in general it's an encouragement not to make lists too long and to concentrate on making each part of a list be sufficiently well-expressed so that it really counts. One telling word is "especially." The notion of asking God to care especially for one child suggests God is as absent-minded and easily distracted as we are. Using the term "especially" is probably a sign that one has introduced too much material and the petition needs pruning.

A third area of verbal repetition can be in "incarnational" prayers where the precise action of God being sought is not specific. Here one can overuse language such as "bless," "be close to," "be with," and "send your Holy Spirit upon"; although, again, finding yourself repeating such terms may be an indication that too much of the wording is imprecise, and the prayer as a whole needs to be re-focused towards the specific action of God.

BEAUTY

The prayers of the people shouldn't set out, in the first instance, to be a thing of beauty. They are a direct address to God, meant for one time and one place, and God is unlikely to be too concerned about the flavor of grammar or style. The important point is to be direct, honest, and succinct, and to express the prayer in such a way that everyone present can say "Amen" at the end. Nonetheless, it's appropriate to speak of a prayer being beautiful, if beauty names a deep resonance, a sense of completeness, a feeling of satisfaction, or an intimation of wholeness, for these are exactly the emotions an appropriate intercession should evoke. After the intercession there should be, in the congregation, a certain sense of relief, a freedom to exhale deeply in trust that something that very much needed to be done has been done. And there may well also be a half-shed tear, a sense that something has been named that is seldom named, a depth plumbed that is usually kept much more superficial, a burden shared that has been habitually carried alone. That is a moment of beauty.

It's appropriate to speak of a prayer being beautiful, if beauty names a deep resonance, a sense of completeness, a feeling of satisfaction, or an intimation of wholeness.

When people refer to the beauty of a prayer, what they are often trying to name is the quality of being drawn deeply into a particular image, the experience of being absorbed in layer after layer of meaning. It's important to remember that less is more. People appreciate being given a particular focus rather than being asked to comprehend a wide range of concerns in a scattershot way. In many ways, prayer is training for learning to rest in the goodness of God. The fourteenth-century mystic Julian of Norwich, who was known for her wisdom on this subject, says, "Rest in the goodness of God. For that goodness reaches to the depths of our needs." The intercessor doesn't have to do a whole lot in prayer to keep God busy or to keep the congregation busy. It is important to be free of that notion. The sense that the prayer needs to be "busy" means it can end up containing too many images or mixed metaphors. It can mean that, in an effort to attain a prayerful mode, the person leading prayers piles up an overabundance of language, florid phrases, and garish verbosity, which, even if poetic, suffocate one another. A prayer that begins "God of the glory of every corner of creation and every unfolding season, you woke us to fresh dew and green grass and refreshed us with rain even though it was a thunderstorm and warmed us with sun and fit us for glory like the blue eternal sky . . ." is already at risk of this overextension. The antidote to overdoing it is finding one or two images and going deep with them, discovering layers of meaning as you go. It might be better to say, "God, who looked over your creation and called it good, give us the grace of rest to enjoy your world in the way you do. . . ."

It's also possible that the prayer never attains a lyric quality at all because the intercessor thinks of the prayer more like an essay than a poem. The sense that the prayer has become an essay also contributes to a feeling of busy-ness in the prayer, because in prose there is little opportunity to pause or to comprehend beyond the surface meaning, while in poetry that possibility reliably exists. In any good poem, there is the surface meaning, and then there is additional meaning found when the listener attunes to what it evokes in her, to its echo in her own life and experience. This is what draws people into a poem: it induces and provokes the readers or hearers to do the most interesting and rewarding work themselves. It is similar with prayer. If the prayer is structured so that there is only the surface meaning, and people don't have an opportunity to interlace their own concerns within the vocabulary used or to let an image echo with all its multiple meanings, the prayer will be flat, lacking depth and devoid of resonance. It will have only one dimension. Clearly, not all writers of intercessory prayer are poets, but there are simple ways to give the prayer a poetic quality in its very structure, namely symmetry and balance.

BALANCE AND SYMMETRY

It's not necessary to keep a poetic symmetry of petitions, all clipped to a certain length and style, but if carefully crafted, the prayers of the people are likely to develop their own symmetry and shape. If there are three or four petitions, God may be addressed in each in ways that fit well with the content of the petition and sit well with one another. Thus "God of the past . . . ," "God of the present . . . ," and "God of the future" or "Glorious God . . . ," "Gracious God . . . ," "Gregarious God . . . ," and "Generous God." If such symmetry is hard to articulate, it's always possible to let a scripture passage or a song do it for you — "Maker, in Whom We Live" is one of many hymns that begins each verse with a symmetrical address to God and adapts well to intercessory use; all the better if the one chosen is one of the assigned hymns for the day.

Likewise, a continuous theme can run through each petition while inviting different content. For example, at Christmas each petition can reflect the nature of a journey. One petition can speak of the journey of Mary and Joseph, and pray for migrant populations, expectant parents, and those who face danger; a second can refer to the journey of the shepherds, and name all who sleep outside, face ostracism in their communities, or care for animals in any way; a third can recall the magi, and intercede for scholars, all who live in the lands to the east of Bethlehem, and any who know what it means to walk a long way to Jerusalem but find themselves in the wrong place; while a fourth can remember the journey of God from heaven to earth, and mention those who need God to be with them in places of fear, bitterness, hunger, and despair. In this way intercession enriches and reflects the reading of the familiar story, while peopling that story with a wide range of contemporary characters, all within a cohesive, succinct, and memorable shape.

Similar issues arise regarding the related question of balance. Balance means keeping the ship afloat and not going overboard in one direction or another. It means not going overboard in terms of political and social commitments: God is the God of the poor and the rich; the prayers of the people should be a place where we gently name the poverty of those we call rich as well as identify the wealth among those we tend to call poor. It means not going overboard with regard to perpetrators and victims of crime: it is almost always possible to focus on those who have been injured, hurt, or bereaved while still leaving a place for God's concern towards the perpetrators and those related to them. It means not going overboard in relation to theological or liturgical vocabulary or taste: in a situation of acute or chronic distress, one is always looking for a change of heart and mind on the part of the influential and visible; but that prayer can always be phrased in such a way that accepts there is more than one understanding of how God instills faith and what form God wants that faith to take. It means not going overboard in terms of how social change occurs: not assuming government is the source of all good or all evil, but highlighting groups in civil society and seeking their strengthening and empowerment and wise conduct.

RESPONSES AND CONCLUSIONS

While variety, spontaneity, imagination, creativity, and scriptural grounding are all virtues in the prayers of the people, they cease to be so when it comes to congregational responses. Why? Because the intercessor is leading people before the face of God in a period of concentration, focus, trust, compassion, self-involvement, presence, and devotion. The last thing that's needed in such a moment is a complex, original, elaborate response that breaks the attention and sends the people scurrying for a bulletin or mouthing a half-remembered exchange that only begins to lodge in the memory once the final petition is done. The whole intention of framing the prayers of the people is to arrive at elegant simplicity: over-elaboration dismantles the mood one is seeking to instill. And that over-elaboration is commonly found at the point of congregational responses.

It may seem counterintuitive for a book about interceding to discourage the practice of using weekly-themed prayers from a denominational resource. But everything in this book is intended to help intercessors prepare their own prayers with confidence and grace. It intends to encourage those who pray to write their own prayers suitable for the time and place. The danger in adopting prayers — including those supplied by formal denominational resources — is that it encourages people to bypass the two foundational forms of preparation — familiarity with the scriptural themes and engagement with events and trends in the contemporary world. Scripture leads us to God, and shapes how we think about and speak with God; contemporary events and trends provide us with what we talk about. Theological reflection — of the kind found in chapter one of this book — should help us focus on what most matters and what we think we are doing; in other words, it should help us keep things simple, rather than induce us into making things too elaborate. In that sense, the reformation impulse that first led to the Pastoral Prayer — offering a prayer that addressed in detail the local community and congregation, rather than employing previously printed prayers week to week — lies beneath what this book is trying to encourage and strengthen as a practice in the church.

> **The whole intention of framing the prayers of the people is to arrive at elegant simplicity.**

A congregational response is helpful to break up the petitions, maintain the congregation's concentration, and enable the congregation genuinely to "own" each dimension of the prayer. One of the most commonly used and familiarly recognized is "Lord, in your mercy, **hear our prayer.**" But anything that enhances the response beyond that takes energy and focus away from the petition itself — and anything that requires attention to be directed to the details of the response distracts from the petition such as to undermine it almost altogether. In this category come almost all forms of musical response. Music is its own form of prayer, and songs, hymns, and chants can offer profound forms of intercession, but they are in a different vein to the spoken word, and the change of gear does as much to break a mood as to deepen it. There's certainly a place for rhythmic chanting, such as the music of Taizé, to replace conventional spoken intercession altogether in some circumstances — but interspersed with the spoken word, it tends to inhibit rather than emphasize that spoken word. Again, over-elaboration diminishes the result. The congregation should be induced into a condition where someone — the intercessor — is doing something "for" them, with their full consent and participation, in a way that makes them deeply grateful and requires their full attention. It's a little bit like having one's hair cut: you can't do it yourself, you need it to be done, and the doing of it may be very satisfying. But it's best not to be distracted by lots of extra things going on at the same time.

It's best to stick with the best-known response in your congregation. For many people that will be "Lord, in your mercy, **hear our prayer**." We might want to say more — "**hear our prayer, and respond, anticipating your kingdom and building up your church**"; but that would be to go beyond the category of response and to re-enter the language of petition itself. It would be to seek to do more than a response needs to do, and to distract from the petition itself. One possible exception might be to adopt a simple quotation from a hymn. Thus, in times of trouble, where it is hard to know exactly what to ask God to do besides be present and bring comfort, one might consider the response "The darkness deepens — **Lord, with us abide**." This has all the advantages noted in chapter three about incorporating hymns, but it still has serious disadvantages, not least that remembering the response (let alone picking up a bulletin to locate that response and be reassured it doesn't change each time) is more than enough to distract most members of the congregation from the content and process of the petitions themselves. The only context where the advantages of a response like this outweigh the disadvantages is that of the ecumenical gathering, where to use a familiar response either isn't possible, because there is no such thing in this setting, or is undesirable, since it might suggest one denomination's practice was the norm, which is precisely what ecumenical worship tries to avoid doing; yet everyone present might be expected to recognize the words of the hymn "Abide with Me."

When it comes to concluding the intercessions, the person leading has a responsibility to signal clearly to the congregation that the prayer is drawing to a close. There is a choice here between a more standard ending and one that ties together the prayer with the themes of the service. The more standard ending can take two forms: 1) "In Jesus' name we pray" or 2) a Trinitarian ending. Jesus taught his followers to pray in his name, and so there is nothing wrong with ending a prayer in such a way. The pitfall, and the mistake to avoid at all costs, is tacking on "In Jesus' name we pray" in a perfunctory and abrupt way. When the prayers end with a sudden "In Jesus' name we pray" tacked on after the last petition, the congregation can be jolted, especially if what has preceded has done its work of allowing them to sink into a deep place of prayer. It's terribly disappointing to be in a setting where such an ending conveys the leader's obvious discomfort and unfortunate eagerness to bring the prayer to an end.

The other option for a more standard ending is to conclude with language that explicitly names the Trinity: "All these prayers we ask in the name of Christ Jesus our Lord, who with the Father and Holy Spirit lives and reigns forever. Amen." This approach recognizes the scriptural importance of praying in Jesus' name, but it doesn't seek to fulfill that instruction bluntly. The prayer is addressed to Jesus in the fullness of his relationship with the Father and Holy Spirit. The point of Trinitarian language is not formality for its own sake. Rather, praying in such a way boldly entrusts human cares to the bonds of Father, Son, and Holy Spirit. Moreover, it leaves the people with the sense that their prayers are received into the full presence of God. Its length also clearly signals that the prayers of the people are drawing to a close, preparing the congregation for the transition. Depending upon the overall structure of the prayer, one ending may be more suitable than the other. If the prayer has been addressed to Jesus as Lord, then a Trinitarian ending might be best. If Trinitarian language is present throughout, then a simpler conclusion which addresses Jesus might be preferable.

If the intercessor is seeking to tie together the themes of the conclusion more explicitly with the rest of the service, there are two ways to do this: 1) adapt an existing collect or 2) quote a hymn. Any existing collect that fits appropriately with what has been spoken in the petitions that precede it may provide a satisfying conclusion. Particularly if there is a period of silence preceding the conclusion, the intercessor needs to offer more than a standard ending in order to gather up the prayers which have been offered in the silence and draw the whole time of prayer to an end. Another creative way to tie together the conclusion with the rest of the service is to quote a hymn, perhaps a whole verse, either verbatim or adapted. A hymn included in worship for the day may be particularly evocative. This is perhaps the most effective use of a hymn in the intercessions — a practice that should not be overdone, but which can conclude on a deeply satisfying and sometimes moving note.

In some churches, the Lord's Prayer follows the petitions as the primary opportunity for congregational response in the midst of prayer, and if so, the intercessor bears the responsibility of making this transition and needs to signal clearly to the people that their verbal participation is needed. Assuming their eyes have been closed in prayer, they are not looking at the bulletin to see what is coming next, so the intercessor must give verbal cues that a shift is coming. For example, "All these prayers we ask in the name of Jesus our Lord who prays with us, Our Father. . . ." This type of ending is very common in settings that employ a Pastoral Prayer, which in its most comprehensive form often moves through each element of adoration, confession, thanksgiving, supplication and then concludes with the Lord's Prayer. When the Lord's Prayer comes as a conclusion, it typically indicates there is not a Eucharist to follow, and so the unison ending serves an even further purpose of uniting the gathered body as one.

SILENCE

Silence and extempore prayer have been saved to the end for a number of reasons. One, because they are in some sense the goal of the prayers of the people; the individuals who have had prayers offered to God on their behalf should be better able to be silent and to offer prayers on their own behalf. Two, because silence and extempore prayer, when conducted in the context of public worship, need just as much care and consideration as more formal petitions do, and by elaborating on what that care and consideration consists in for such petitions, this book has sought to indicate what such preparation for silence and extempore prayer might mean. Three, and closely related to the first two, the practice of preparing intercessions should begin with silence and extempore prayer.

Speech is silence interrupted by sound. Communication is only partly about words: much of the real interaction takes place in non-verbal ways. The intercessor is leading people into the presence of God, and even in a public gathering, much of what is taking place

> Silence and extempore prayer, when conducted in the context of public worship, need just as much care and consideration as more formal petitions do.

is each person coming before God with his or her own concerns and pleas. What the intercessor is doing is providing a framework for that to take place — a framework that is valid in itself without the silences being filled, but a framework that can facilitate something even more profound and significant.

How is this done? First of all by employing resonant phrases which leave space for the members of the congregation to amplify and illustrate from their own circle of acquaintance. Part of this is not being too specific or prescriptive. Imagine the aftermath of a massacre in a school, park, or shopping center. Consider the difference between "Send your Holy Spirit upon all who have become lost in a cycle of violence and revenge," and "Guide the hand of lawmakers to ban handguns." The prayers of the people are not the place for the nuanced framing of public policy. The careful intercessor will offer a compassionate phrase that has an application beyond the immediate context, both so that it is clear that this is about shared pain rather than passing judgment on the foolish or perverse, and so that the congregation can fill the silence with other experiences of violence and ceaseless revenge.

It's important to avoid using language that's too vivid or technical. Such terminology closes down the imagination and the frame of reference and can be distracting or even distressing. For example the terms "abuse," "anorexia," and "pregnancy" are too explicit. Much better to use more open and suggestive terms such as the following: "all for whom home is a place of fear"; "any who have come to regard food as an enemy"; "those who are facing the promise or prospect of new life within them or around them." This is not simply a matter of squeamishness around certain words, or a desire not to offend or expose: it's more to ensure the silence that follows the words is full of a dynamic range of possible understandings, rather than a narrower, medicalized scope of expertise and insider knowledge. It's important to mention mental illness frequently, to balance the tendency to focus entirely on physical conditions; but again it's best to speak in more allusive terms, such as "be close to any who wake each morning wondering how they will get through the day."

The simplest way to make the most of silence is to recognize that most people on most Sundays will come to church with particular persons or issues pressing on their hearts, and unless and until they have a place to "park" those thoughts, they won't be able fully to engage the rest of the liturgy. The best place to receive that pressing concern is in the prayers of the people; and the simplest way to do so is to have an intentional period of silence shaped for exactly that purpose. It's good if such a moment can arise naturally out of one of the petitions that follow the theme of the day — because one would hope that what has been heard in readings and sermon will have shed some light on the pressing issue. But it's important that the silence be offered in very general terms, so almost any concern can find a home in it. Thus, "In a moment of silence we seek your blessing upon those whom we long to help but don't know how to . . . ," or "Be close to all who are struggling this week and whom we now name in the silence of our hearts." It should be quite possible to create a new form of words each week that does justice to the petitions and the theme while paying attention to current events and remaining sufficiently general to be open to almost any struggle the members of the congregation might be dealing with.

A lecturer likes to believe that the audience enjoys a lecture because of the brilliance of the argument and the depth and quality of the illustrations. A performer likes to believe that the audience applauds because of the dexterity and imagination of the performance. But the truth is that audiences respond because of the things beyond the lecture or performance that the event triggers in their imaginations or unlocks in their memories. The same is true of intercessions. The words offered are to a great degree a ladder that falls away if and when the members of the congregation are brought face to face with the living God. It's not that the words are unimportant: the whole intent is to make the words ones of a depth of epic and lyric description that gives the congregation complete confidence that this is an encounter with God to which they can entrust their whole soul. But once that soul is entrusted, the words are largely keeping the conversation on track: the conversation itself is between the believer and God.

The words offered are to a great degree a ladder that falls away if and when the members of the congregation are brought face to face with the living God.

EXTEMPORE PRAYER

Why go to all this trouble? Why not simply invite people to pray spontaneously and allow the Holy Spirit to form the words in them as they go along?

Because seeking the great can too often inhibit reaching the good. Extempore prayer is, in very many ways, the ideal. There's a quality to the present, to the immediate, to the voice that's not bound to a script and to a heart that's entirely in the now and not stuck in the ideas of a day or two ago. The summit of human experience is to be able to stand before God and converse with God; if one's conversation is shaped by good habits, laced with scriptural resonances, informed by God's own manner of speech, so much the better; if it is true to your own character, good in its integrity and transparency, and beautiful in its simplicity of desire, better still. To be swept up in the spirit of extempore prayer is an experience of head and heart in full accord, of soul in tune with body, of all of one's existence being present and in communion with God. It doesn't get better than that.

In personal settings there is no substitute for extempore prayer. By the bedside, at a time of crisis, before a meeting, with a child, before a meal: in such places a "prepared statement" generally feels unnatural, wooden, whereas a weaving together of circumstance and cherished revelation, in intimate and tender language, evokes depth and worship and trust. In public worship there can be a unique element to extempore prayer — it is, for example, much more suited to the kind of dwelling on individual words, the turning them over from various angles like an uncut diamond, the repetition and underlining of certain poignant phrases, that we earlier explored as similar to the practice of *lectio divina*. Thus, in a confession of sin when the reading is Genesis 3, the leader may say God's words to Adam and Eve, "Where are you?", in various ways with differing valences, or if the reading is 1 Kings 19, the leader may say God's words to Elijah at Horeb, "What are you doing here?", in a similar meditative tone. The tone of voice is almost everything. Such a mood is invariably lost if one is using a prepared script.

But that doesn't mean such prayer is completely spontaneous: on the contrary, it has doubtless had just as careful preparation as a formal script — simply without being written down. The ideal is probably to have someone able to lead worship who knows the scripture and the liturgy so well and is so deft in her or his theological and pastoral judgments and so poetic in her or his use of language that prayer can be improvised in the moment based on careful meditation for hours beforehand. To be a worshiper in such a setting is a truly wonderful experience. But such people and such circumstances are rare — so rare that we're assuming this is almost never the circumstance and this book need not address it. In more regular circumstances, extempore prayer in public worship is likely to be a cover for under-preparation, an excuse for returning to predictable and well-worn categories, or an opportunity to discover a little too much of the intercessor's uncensored personal agenda.

The truth is that extempore prayer, so often taken to be a sign of the unconstrained movement of the Holy Spirit, a marinating in the wine of the kingdom, is too often among the most overplayed and tired forms of liturgy. (And let's not pretend it isn't liturgical; it has its own rules and traditions as much as any other form of prayer.) If you haven't prepared what to say, you generally end up saying the kinds of things you usually say; if you usually don't prepare what you say, you will usually say the same things every time; if you say the same things every time, they'll doubtless be a collection of half-remembered *bon mots* and underdeveloped promising configurations and somewhat poorly expressed genuine insights. All of which are quite adequate for personal prayer, if sincere and delivered with integrity, but if this is the central moment of this congregation's week, and if you have been set aside, like Zechariah in Luke 1, to go within the veil and commune with God on the people's behalf, don't God and the people deserve a little better? Don't they deserve you to find the most acute words you can and focus on the most pressing issues in the world and put them in relation to your very best understanding of the import of the day's scriptures in the light of your best attempt to coordinate with your colleagues in leading the liturgy that day? If you say "God doesn't mind," then why have corporate prayer at all — why not just let the congregation articulate their own in an extended period of silence? If you say, "The congregation isn't looking for an expert," why take any extra care over publicly spoken words at all? Let us be clear: when done well, extempore prayer is the best tradition of all; but when done badly, it becomes a veil for laziness of liturgy or theology.

Like all liturgy, carefully-constructed and thoughtfully-delivered inter-cessions are a form of training. A congregation that has listened to and shared such prayers should, over a period of time, have learned the ca-dences and rhythms so well that they can reproduce them as the occasion demands. The extempore prayer that formal petitions are looking to evoke is not the dramatic event in the course of the liturgy, but the more inti-mate, yet transformative moment at the hospital bedside, at the roadside accident site, on receipt of bad news, at a crossroads moment in a family's life — when one person, or many, comfortable in the shape of a collect, mindful of how God has worked before, clear about what they want to ask God for, with a sense of what an answered prayer might look like, takes hold of the moment, makes eye contact with everyone in the group, and says, quietly, but boldly, perhaps for the first time in their life, "Friends, this is a difficult time. Let us pray: Tender God, you watched your Son's agony on the cross; look with mercy on your children here before you in our distress. Come among us now. . . ."

SIX

Examples: Seasons

ADVENT

(1)

God of glory, your prophet Isaiah prayed that you would tear the heavens and come down. Come down today, that your hungry people may find food and may find their hunger deeply met in you; that your faithless people may see you face to face and find their hope restored; that your lonely people may find companions for their journey and know in you a companion who will never leave them alone; that your grieving people may find a shoulder to share their sorrow and speak with you the words of eternal life; that your angry people may find in you a fire greater than their own and a passion deeper than justice; that your despairing people may find a reason to live and in you see a beauty beyond beholding; that your tired people may find strength to go on and in you find rest for their souls. Bring the hope of your coming kingdom to the fears of Mumbai, of Nigeria, of Wall Street, of Kabul, of Baghdad. In a moment of quiet we ask you to tear the heavens and come down in a place or circumstance where we know not what might be for the best.

* * *[1]

---

1. Asterisks indicate the space for a congregational response in churches where that is the practice or, in the absence of that, a silent pause. In many of these prayers, "Lord, in your mercy, **hear our prayer**" was the congregational response.

Come, thou long expected Jesus, born to set thy people free; from our fears and sins release us, let us find our rest in thee. God of wonder and joy, in your Son's second coming you save the best until last. Fix our eyes on the form of his appearing, that we may see the wounds his dazzling body bears and in them know the wounds we seek to nurse in one another and fear to reveal in ourselves. Let us know those who set at naught and sold him, pierced and nailed him to the tree, that we may perceive where terrible crimes take place today, that we may be among those who repent and regret and bewail and lament, and that we may know when it is we who have perpetrated or abetted those crimes through economic interest or political force or social neglect. Give us grace to discover what it means to gaze on those glorious scars with rapture, and so empower us to look back on our own scars, our hurts, our bitterness, our regrets, our failures, or betrayals, and our wounds, and see them transformed by the scars of your Son, so that each scar be a point of entry to your broken body, each nail mark a binding to your sacrifice of love, and each thorn-wound an anticipation of your crown of glory; in you who reigned from the tree and now reigns forever, world without end. Amen.

This intercession has only two petitions; in fact they are really one long petition with a single theme, broken up by a single congregational response. The second petition weaves the words of two Advent hymns, "Come, Thou Long-Expected Jesus" and "Lo, He Comes with Clouds Descending," to offer an extended appeal to God to reshape the church in the image of Christ.

---

(2)

Passionate God, your Son Jesus went out to meet John in the wilderness; come out today and meet us in our wilderness. Where one of your children is a long way from home, make yourself known to them in their long lonely exile; where another is a long way from where they recognize they should be in spirit and in truth, show them the way they should go and give them truthful and patient companions to walk the way with them; where your people are hungry and without resources, make the wilderness a place of discovery and fruitfulness, bringing refreshment from heaven and gushing nourishment from underground; and where one among your sheep is lonely and isolated, bring them a deeper love of your creation, a surer trust in the simple texture of life, and a more intimate embrace with your own heart.

✳   ✳   ✳

Faithful God, your Son Jesus went out to meet John in his wildness; come out today and meet us in our wildness. Where one of us lives with mental scars, give us courage to step into the unknown, hope to walk alongside, and personal and professional help to get through each day; where another lives with dementia, give us beautiful gestures where words fail, and endurance to sustain the long haul; where your people live with the damage of a moment of madness, give them your Holy Spirit to repair and restore and reconcile and heal; and where we struggle to live with the wildness in ourselves, inspire us to love ourselves as you love us, to shape our lives according to your hopes for us, and to recognize our humanity as cherished by you. In a moment of quiet we offer you the wildness in our own hearts that you may come to meet us there.

✳   ✳   ✳

Liberating God, in Isaiah you prophesied that your servant would be anointed by your spirit; as you promised to bring good news to those in debt, be with all who open their mail each day to face figures of despair; as you promised to bind up the brokenhearted, be close to those who are devastated in love, betrayed in trust, or bereaved in hope; as you promised to proclaim liberty to the oppressed, be among the ones who live in daily fear, under tyrannical regimes, in dangerous neighborhoods, or under the thunderous gaze of a member of their own family; as you promised to release the prisoners, be with those incarcerated, all facing trial, and any on death row.

✳   ✳   ✳

Saving God, in Jesus you went into the exile of abandonment, agony, and death for no other reason than that you loved us at the heart of your being. Make us people who love the way you love, that even if our lives encounter wilderness and pain, others may know that when they meet us, they meet your passion in our every touch and sound and tenderness. In Jesus' name. Amen.

Here there is an interplay between wilderness and wildness in engaging the lyric dimensions of John the Baptist. It's important that wildness isn't simply something that happens among "them," but is assumed to be a part of the congregation's experience. The phrase "under the thunderous gaze of a member of their own family" gives a hint of a way to talk about issues of domestic abuse.

—————

(3)

God of surprises, in your angel Gabriel you came and interrupted the life of Mary, the life of Israel, and the life of the world. Be close to all whose routine has been disrupted by war, by horror, by terror, by disaster; sustain those whose educational or commercial hopes have been displaced by financial crisis, sudden uncertainty, or unforeseen crisis; and fill the hearts of any who are surprised by joy, impatient as the wind, thrilled with new faith, new love, new reason to live in you. Make us, Lord, so eager to enter your presence that we may cherish the interruptions of your Holy Spirit, such that even in hostile interruptions we may yet find disclosures of your grace, and find in the interruption of death an entry to true peace.

*   *   *

Mysterious God, whose servant Paul spoke of the revelation of that which was kept secret for long ages; be close to all those whose lives are interlaced with secrets. For people whose professional calling entails holding secrets that are hard to bear, we ask for strength and forbearance; for all whose work for their country requires handling official secrets, we pray for honor and integrity; for those for whom each day is a maze of deception to cover up what they fear to be discovered about who they are or what they've done, we plead for compassion, grace, and truth; and for any who are burdened by the weight of secrets that are not their own, we ask for wisdom, patience, and courage.

* * *

Everlasting God, you promised through your prophet Nathan that the throne of David would be established forever. Be close to all who have discovered that what they thought was forever may in fact not be. Comfort those who feel betrayed in love, in business, in friendship, in neighborhood and family life; strengthen all who have made promises they now feel or suspect or know that they cannot keep; and send your grace on those facing the ache and loss of bereavement, the discomfort and dismay of sickness, and the shame and distress of unemployment. Be with those who have no place to call home, all who don't know where they will sleep tonight, and for every person who has no one they can truly call a friend.

* * *

God of wonders and signs, whose servant Mary said, "How can this be?"; we acknowledge before you how little we understand, how often we doubt, and how reluctant we are to trust your ways. In a moment of silence we place in your hands one thing we believe you have promised but that just now seems far out of sight. . . . Give us faith that remembers and treasures how you have acted before, trusts and expects that you will act again, and waits with longing and desire for every step you take, that we might be your Advent people, in whose hearts are your highways and whose every step draws ourselves and others nearer, our Lord, to thee. Amen.

This is a prayer for the Fourth Sunday in Advent; it begins with Mary but explores wider themes of promises kept and promises broken. The use of quotation is much less explicit and more allusive — "surprised by joy," "nearer, our Lord, to thee." There is a particular effort to interweave epic matters concerning economic adversity with lyric concerns of betrayal and desire.

CHRISTMAS

(1)

Loving God, in your Son Jesus Christ, you show us the nature and destiny of your creation and salvation;

Bless [this church], stable of strangers and angels, and continue to make this a community that seeks to reflect your glory and humility;

Bless [this city], city of honest human endeavor and unresolved human struggle, and continue to make it a community where your word is made flesh;

Bless your church throughout the world, and be close to everyone who celebrates your Son's birth this holy season;

Bless those people and places that long to hear the angels' message of peace and goodwill;

Most of all, bless those who, like the holy family, have no place to stay, no security to rely on, and are strangers and pilgrims on earth;

And finally bless those with whom we have shared Christmases past, and with whom, in glory, we long to share Christmas again, because of your Son, who came to live with us, that we might forever live with you. Amen.

A carol service is an occasion for letting word and music say most of what needs to be said. Prayers can be brief: but the occasion is so drenched in personal and theological meaning that they can be direct and make close connections between abiding themes and harsh realities. A degree of traditional language makes sharp words easier to hear.

(2)

Lord God, who came down to earth from heaven, day by day, like us you grew. Once a child so dear and gentle, now our Lord in heaven above, bless the children who have gathered here to sing tonight. Shepherd us into the joy of Christmas by their song of faith to you. Christ our Lord, our infant king, welcome us all as your children around your manger and lead us on to the place where you have gone, that at last our eyes shall see you through your own redeeming love. Amen.

This prayer is for a local church children's choir Christmas concert. It uses resonant phrases from "Once in Royal David's City." The phrasing changes slightly from the language of the hymn (third person) to second person in order to address God directly. This is an example of how a hymn can be rewoven into the form of a collect.

(3)

Holy God, newborn child, in whom heaven and earth meet, draw us near to you, to kneel at your manger. Keep us close to you to enjoy the awe and wonder of your birth. In the freshness of your newborn life, give courage to all of us who want to begin again, all who need a fresh start, and all who long for the freedom of your forgiveness. Give your mercy to us who are weary and look for a place to rest in your presence. Renew us as heaven and earth meet, that we may find our true life in you and with you, even now, even here.

* * *

Jesus our shepherd king, who was visited by shepherds keeping watch, tend us as your flock. As you were visited by the wise men from the East, be our king to govern with compassion and mercy.

Make your church a sanctuary for sheep who have wandered and strayed. Create among us your kingdom of peace, which cannot be toppled or destroyed or overthrown. Hold fast the Holy Land where you lived and Bethlehem where you were born and all places around our world where peace seems far away.

* * *

God of Mary and Joseph, who welcomed the greetings of angels, inspire our hearts with sure trust in your promises. Bless all who are far from home this Christmas. Comfort all who have lost loved ones this past year. Come close to all who cannot be together with the ones they hold most dear on this day of joy. Pour your grace upon those who suffer from sickness, and those who are lonely and hurting. Send your heavenly host to visit us as we are, dear Lord. By your Holy Spirit lift us up by the healing in your wings and make our hearts sing the song of angels in the starry skies. Amen.

Christmas Day worship is full of joy, but there is a place in intercessions to name places where strife remains. It is a day to pray for the places named in the story of Jesus' birth and to mention by name Bethlehem and the surrounding area. Pastorally speaking, there are plenty of places in people's lives where struggle persists on Christmas Day. The intercessions are an opportunity to name such concerns, within a worship service whose overall tone is one of rejoicing.

EPIPHANY

(1)

God of gold, your Son's glory was proclaimed in the magi's first gift, and your name is made known in the abundance of the sea and the wealth of nations; be among the kings and rulers of your world, that they may be gentle shepherds like you. Give every principal, leader, or chief executive a searching heart like the wise men, that they may be quick to ask advice, ready to realize when they are wrong, and willing to retrace their steps by a different path. As the three kings came to bear your Son homage, give us grace to bear homage to those people and in those places that embody your spirit and speak of your glory. Make this church such a place in this new year.

* * *

God of frankincense, your Son's holiness was declared in the magi's second gift, and your presence is thrilling and radiant; live in all who seek your call, your will, and your blessing. Strengthen those whose lives are given to the search for truth. Build them up in their scholarship and teaching. Walk with those who find your ways hard to understand, in the midst of sickness, disappointment, loneliness, or fear. In a moment of silence we bring to you one place where we ask you to show your will for us in the year to come. . . . Make us a people who will search the skies for you, cross the desert for you, and bow down and worship you wherever you may be found.

* * *

God of myrrh, your Son's call to suffer was anticipated in the magi's third gift, and your Son while still young himself became a refugee from persecution; live in the bodies, minds, and spirits of those whose lives are poured out on the altar of suffering. Be a home to all who enter the new year homeless: be the pillow for their weary head, the shoes for their worn-out feet, the friend for their lonely heart; and give them companions who can accompany them on the road to self-respect, stability of life, dignity, and service to others. Lord, you know the ways we are homeless. Call to us across the desert of our bewilderment, shine your star in the night sky of our fear, and bring us to the place where your tenderness, your intimacy, and your living presence are to be found.

* * *

Teach us, Lord, to follow your star to where you lie; to admit when we've lingered in the wrong place; to recognize you, even in a stable; and when we have worshiped you, to go away new people walking a new path of glory, holiness, and suffering for the life of your world. Amen.

When the central story of the day offers such a compelling threefold shape, it's a simple matter to design intercessions that adopt that shape. These are prayers for Epiphany itself; there's not much in life that can't find a place under the headings of gold, frankincense, and myrrh. Here a specially composed final prayer aims to sum up the spirit of the whole celebration.

----

(2)

God of passion and compassion, in your servant Paul you give us five ways to prepare for the coming of your kingdom. You say, "Let even those who have wives be as though they had none": give hope to those for whom marriage is a source not of joy but despair, not of companionship and up-building but of loneliness and humiliation, not of tenderness and trust but of rejection and betrayal. Give grace to the single, and to all who experience singleness as a burden. And give wisdom to all who don't know how to reconcile their love and longing with their fear, their resentment, or their guilt.

*   *   *

You say, "Let those who mourn be as though they were not mourning": be with all who watch a loved one die, and any who get sudden news that shreds their heart. Sustain your children for whom every day seems a walk into the unknown of grief and bewilderment. Encourage those who know they are facing the reality of their own death, and give us all ears to hear the unutterable words and friendships that hold out when words fail.

*   *   *

88

You say, "Let those who rejoice be as though they were not rejoicing":
bless all who went to Washington, DC, on Tuesday, that the excite-
ment of welcoming a new president may become in the power of your
Spirit courage to take steps of faith and commitment to encounter
you in the places you tell us you are to be found. Give discernment to
those who seek to discover how to meet and serve you in politics, in
their regular career, in their studies, and among your children who
struggle under oppression, distress, or despair.

* * *

You say, "Let those who buy be as though they had no possessions":
raise up all who seek to follow in your footsteps in the way of sim-
plicity and common life. We pray for those called to simplicity of life,
and for all who set an example in relating to the earth; and we recall
before you all whose homes have been repossessed, and have had
simplicity thrust upon them.

* * *

You say, "Let those who deal with the world be as though they had no
dealings with it": empower your servants who seek to mediate and
reconcile in Gaza and Iraq; have mercy on the people of Zimbabwe;
and guide all who strive to shape institutions and relationships that
are invested with your purpose, transfigured by your presence, and
directed by your Spirit.

* * *

Loving God, walk beside us. When we are too hasty, soothe our impa-
tience and anxiety. When we are too tardy, draw us out of our sloth
and bewilderment. And when we are walking step by step with you,
give us grace to look aside to your shoulder, your step, your hand,
that wherever we tread in search or service of you, we may always
know we are not alone. Amen.

This prayer seeks to do more extensive exegetical work — dividing one of the passages (1 Cor. 7:29-31) for the day into five statements and offering a meditation on each one of them. The consequence is five petitions that are more direct and succinct. The mood changes with a more devotional collecting prayer to conclude.

LENT

(1)

Merciful God, teach us to fast. Give us strength to resist our greed and the patience to withstand our passing need. Help us to stand in solidarity with those who don't get to choose. And help us to be hungry for the right things — for righteousness, for justice and peace.

Faithful God, teach us to pray. Give us grace to sit still. Help us to value time with you above all other time. Show us how to find and keep a routine and pattern of life so that you are the ebb and flow of our every thought and word and deed.

Generous God, teach us to give money away. As you have invested your whole destiny in us, let our giving reflect our gratitude and our longing to be like you. Show us the person, the institution, the cause to which you will us to be bound by bonds of finance and affection.

Truthful God, teach us to examine ourselves. Search inside our hearts and take away those things that don't belong there. Help us to search inside your heart and put the things we find there inside our own.

Revealing God, teach us to read your scripture. Show us the parts of your story we forget and open to us the aspects of your purposes we fail to comprehend. Make your Word a lantern to our feet and a light to our path.

Reconciling God, come and heal our broken relationships. This Lent show us one enemy who can become a friend. Introduce us to a stranger who opens to us a window into your kingdom. And teach us when and how to say the word "Sorry." Amen.

This is an intercession for Ash Wednesday. It takes the six devotional acts of Lent and turns them each into a prayer. Ash Wednesday isn't primarily a day for intercession, but for penitence, so the intercessions are suitably brief.

(2)

God our light, your Son Jesus Christ exposes who we truly are; we humbly ask you to lighten our path today. When we cannot see the path ahead, give us a glimpse of your Son beyond the mystery of the unknown. When we fear we have ruined everything, show us the restoring and redeeming face of your forgiveness. When we have nothing left to give, light up our hearts and souls with a joy beyond our desiring. Make us a people who crave your light, bathe in your glory, rejoice in your truth, and long for your full disclosure in the second coming of your Son.

* * *

God our life, you are rich in mercy and raise us up with your Son Jesus Christ; help us to understand and make peace with the urgings of our sexual nature. Come and comfort those for whom sex is a place of hurt, anxiety, and exploitation. Show your vulnerable love to all for whom sex has been impoverished as no more than an instrument of power and self-indulgence. Lord who took human flesh, meet each one of us in the core of our neediness and tenderness, and transform our primal longings into desire for your intimacy, your wondrousness, and your glory.

* * *

God our love, you know our hearts better than we do. Cleanse all whose souls are consumed with anger, and meet us in the anger we fear to name. Be with those whose lives are dominated by conflict and show us your face in any we are reluctant to call but know to be our enemies. Send your Spirit on all whose minds are weighed down by anxiety and drop your still dews of quietness upon the restless places in our spirits. In a moment of quiet we place in the palm of your hand one issue too heavy for us to carry ourselves. . . . Soften our hearts, Lord, to realize the wounds in one another, and teach us to be people of compassion, slow to take offense.

✳ ✳ ✳

Almighty God, you give us the gift of prayer. Shine your light upon those who have no one to pray for them; all who have lost the heart to pray; and any whose faith has ebbed away or never found a home in you. Make our lives a prayer, that every gesture raises up the downtrodden, every sigh searches for your wisdom, and every silence opens us to the imitation of your Son, our savior Jesus Christ. Amen.

Here a more explicit attempt is made to offer symmetry in the beginning and shape of each petition. The second petition is an example of how to incorporate a cycle of prayer without drawing attention to it: the theme for the week concerns sexuality, but it is taken in as broad a sense as possible. The phrase "drop your still dews of quietness" is a nod to the hymn "Dear Lord and Father of Mankind."

(3)

God of love, your Son Jesus emptied himself, and took the form of a slave; be with those who've given without counting the cost, those who've fought and not heeded the wounds, those who've labored and not asked for any reward, save that of knowing that they do your will. Bless all who feel their lives have been poured out and they have nothing left to give; any who've given too much in the past, and now feel reluctant to commit or to risk hurt or rejection; and those who sense their lives are near the end, and their bodies cannot serve like once they did. Be close to all who truly know what it means to be a slave, to a harsh master, to an addiction, or to illness. And make us a people ready to live as you live and love as you love.

* * *

God of patience, your Son Jesus was obedient to the point of death on the cross. Give us the gift of obedience. When we need to stick with a task, a promise, a relationship, show us the small steps that can enable us to do so. When we need to bite our tongue or just keep going at work, at home, or in our walk of faith, give us the grace and dignity to be humble and to persevere. Be with those who suffer because of their love for you, those who face physical danger, economic hardship, or personal discrimination. As you prayed for your persecutors, we now pray for the enemies we name in the silence of our hearts.

* * *

God of joy, your Son Jesus was highly exalted and given the name that is above every name. Bless those whose names are very prominent in our lives, whose decisions affect us deeply, whose good esteem shapes our well-being, whose wisdom guides our uncertain steps. Tend with loving care all who feel paralyzed by an uncertain future, tormented by a painful past, or bewildered in a fragile present. In a moment of silence we commend to you one person or situation that stretches us to a place of vulnerable need. . . . Make us a people of joy, who know no circumstance is below the reach of your cross and no hope is beyond the possibility of your resurrection, through Jesus Christ our Lord. Amen.

On Palm Sunday there's usually much else going on in the service and intercessions generally take a back seat. Here the petitions are woven around the three themes of Philippians 2: the incarnation, the crucifixion, and the exaltation of Christ. Again, any time the scriptural passages offer a three- or fourfold shape, it's a gift not to be missed. The first petition adapts a well-loved prayer of St. Ignatius of Loyola.

EASTER

(1)

Risen Christ, you invited your disciples to touch you. Touch us today. Offer your gentle touch to those who have known harshness, or anger, or brutality, or rejection. Teach us how to touch one another in ways that are a blessing. Inspire us to see how our hands may be your hands, our face may be your face, our presence may be your presence. And make us eager recipients of your touch when it arrives from your messengers and angels, and when it comes in the touch of those often treated as untouchable.

* * *

Prince of Peace, you stood among your disciples and said, "Peace be with you." Give us your peace. Be with young people in our city for whom relationships are fragile, work is uncertain, and violence is a constant fear or temptation. Be among the people of southern Sudan, of Sri Lanka, and of Lebanon, and all places where peace is a memory and a dream. Speak now to the place in our own lives that we keep carefully hidden because we are at war with ourselves or with others or with you. . . . And may your blessing begin right there.

* * *

Glorious Savior, your disciples were terrified at your appearance. Teach us through those who terrify us and through the fear that arises from our own ignorance or prejudice. Deepen our joy in human life by our greater understanding of diversity of language and customs. As we ponder the mystery and wonder of humankind, lift our hearts with praise that you became like us, and make our deepest longing to be like you.

* * *

Ascended Lord, even as the disciples celebrated your resurrection they prepared for your departure on high. Give grace to those in the midst of difficult endings and departures and farewells. Be close to those for whom this community has been a blessing like they have never known before, and a place it is hard to leave. Be with all who are leaving yet feel something important remains unfinished. And embrace any who are staying yet feel the most significant relationship or goal is not here. Help us, Lord, when we know we need to let go, and give us faith in your promise that you will never let us go. Amen.

The Easter season coincides with the final weeks of the college year. There's lots of opportunity to blend the themes of Jesus preparing to leave his disciples with students preparing to graduate. It's somewhat harder to link the Easter themes with more epic, global concerns, without sounding trite: here a connection is made with the general notion of peace.

———

(2)

Christ of the empty tomb, who in your glorious resurrection appeared to your disciples locked away in fear, come among us and breathe your renewing Spirit. Where we are locked up by our fears, come and show us your gentle strength. When we are bound by anxiety, come and show us your abundant patience. In the places we are locked behind old hurts, come and help us find the freedom to love again. Make us ready to welcome the peace you bring, ready to extend the forgiveness you share, and ready to go where you send us.

* * *

Christ of wounds, whose hands and side revealed the scars of death, lead us by your Spirit into the promise of life. Hold in your hands those dear to us who are at the edge of death and those struggling with poor health. Wrap your mercy around our loved ones who have recently died, and their families and friends. Comfort our brothers and sisters in places around the world where the wounds of death are all too familiar: the people of Afghanistan, the people of Libya, and the people of Iraq. Christ of the cross, by whose wounds we are healed, make your mercy known in the places in need of healing that are as close as our own hearts, our own families, our own community. And make that same mercy known in the places in need of healing that are farther away: places broken by violence, places torn by fear, and places suffering from loss of life. Through your Holy Spirit, reveal the power of your resurrection and the promise of life in the very midst of the scars of death.

✳   ✳   ✳

Christ of doubting Thomas, who wanted to see and to touch the marks of the nails, give us courage to live as your disciples. Give us the desire to question and to ask and to seek; save us from complacency in our faith that no longer seeks you with our whole heart. In the power of your Spirit, draw near to those who long for faith. Come close to all of us who yearn for the assurance of your presence. Walk beside all who need your nearness now more than ever. Pour out your grace to strengthen your church throughout the world. Inspire us to seek our risen Lord among the wounded places of this world, that finding you there we may ourselves be renewed and that touching the wounds we too may be reborn into the resurrection life.

✳   ✳   ✳

We pray in the name of Christ our Lord who lives with the Father and the Holy Spirit, one God now and forever. Amen.

This prayer uses an extended metaphor about wounds and scars to bring about focused attention. It is a meditation about the wounds in the risen Christ which allows the congregation to imagine how places scarred by death become the site of resurrection. Instead of focusing on the doubts of Thomas, the prayer focuses on the fleshly resurrection of Jesus, in the spirit of incarnation.

(3)

Resurrecting Lord, your Son met the disciples on the first Easter eve-
ning, and returned to meet Thomas a week later. Be with all who, like
Thomas, are looking for a second chance; a second chance to believe, in
longing to see you and to touch you; a second chance to be trusted, in
yearning to find forgiveness and deeper relationship; a second chance
to study, when courses or results have gone awry; a second chance to
work, when a job has gone wrong or been taken away; a second chance
to live, on the other side of an operation; a second chance to live, on
the other side of incarceration. Make us, Lord, a church of the second
chance, that asks questions like Thomas and finds answers in you.

✳ ✳ ✳

Sharing Lord, in the power of your Spirit your Son's first followers had
all things in common; make this church, this town, and this nation
glad in the abundance of the things we hold in common. Bless the
work of nonprofits in our city, and strengthen all who work at low
wages for the common good and strive that there be no needy person
among us. Fill the churches of our city with your Holy Spirit, that all
may see your hand at work in one another and lend support as any
have need. Heal the chasms in our politics and the hatred in our
hearts, that we may truly be one people under you and pledge alle-
giance to your way, your truth, and your life.

✳ ✳ ✳

Forgiving Lord, your Son breathed on the apostles and said, "Peace
be with you." Make your church a people of forgiveness and recon-
ciliation in Syria, in Korea, and in South Sudan. Give your people
courage to listen humbly and speak truthfully about sexuality, about
ecology, about health inequality, about immigration, about guns.
Lend your grace to all who find themselves in the midst of litigation
or intractable disputes. In a moment of silence we recall before you
one conflict we have hidden or withdrawn from that you may be
calling us to rethink or re-engage.

* * *

When peace, like a river, attendeth our way, when sorrows like sea billows roll; whatever our lot, thou has taught us to say, it is well, it is well, with our soul. In the name of Christ. Amen.

The temptation with Thomas is to get too deeply into issues of faith and doubt, which aren't truly the territory of intercession. The way each petition addresses God is designed to offer a more rounded portrayal of the Easter message. Here again a verse of a hymn provides a stirring finale.

---

(4)

Loving shepherd, you have given us refuges of safety. Bless the places that have been sheepfolds for us. Send your loving mercy on your children who have no sheepfold; those who never feel safe. Reach out your arm of mercy to those people left outside our own sheepfold. Bless all for whom this country looks like a sheepfold with a very high wall around it; and those who see this community in a similar way. Make us, Lord, people who seek out sheep of another fold and know those sheep by name.

* * *

Nourishing shepherd, you have given us places of nurture and refreshment. Continue to sustain and nourish the places of good pasture and still waters in our lives. Bless those who worry that life outside this community won't be a verdant meadow, and be with all who are finding goodbyes hard to say. Make this church a place of nurture and refreshment, that here the troubled may find paths of righteousness, and the weary may find restoration for their soul. Strengthen those who strive each day to make their place of work, their institution, their neighborhood, their household places of nurture and refreshment for others, and be close to all who today feel discouraged, disillusioned, or tired at heart.

98

* * *

Faithful shepherd, you come to find us in places of danger, and you walk with us through the valley of the shadow of death. Be close to those faced with fear and panic in the face of the flu virus. Give courage to all who look to the future and count the days. Strengthen any who live each moment without the person in whom their heart rests. Cherish the children and families of those who are incarcerated, and all who are lonely, bewildered, fearful, and ostracized.

* * *

Searching shepherd, you know us and call us by name. When we hide from you, come and find us. When we are lost, track us down. When we are limping or in pain, set us on your shoulders, make us feel your touch and your confidence, and bring us home to you. When like the ordinary shepherd we want to run away, give us what we need to stay still. Make us a people whose lives lie in the palm of your hand, whose relationships are infused with the breath of your Spirit, and whose setbacks become windows for your grace, that we may never cease to wonder at how much you love us, and others may see us and wonder at what your love can do. Amen.

This is a straightforward meditation on Jesus as the good shepherd, blending imagery from John 10 and Psalm 23. Three scenes present themselves — the place of safety, the place of nurture, the place of danger; and a final collect ties all the themes together.

———

(5)

God of glory, in your Son Jesus Christ you love us to the end. Show us the many faces of your love. You have promised that you will be with your people always, and we will be your home. Give us grace to be with those who frighten us, or hurt us, or enrage us, or bore us, and give us words to say, gestures to make, or strength to keep silent, just as you remain present with us however exasperating you must find us. In a moment of quiet we bring before you one person with whom we find it hard to be present, and ask your Holy Spirit to give us whatever it takes to stay still. . . . At the same time we recognize those we yearn to be present to us. Help us find ways to be with people who can't be physically close to us.

* * *

God of Alpha and Omega, you promise that on the last day there will be a new earth. Bless those who renew your earth and our concern for it today. Uphold and strengthen those most closely affected by the oil spillage in the Gulf — all who work in the oil industry and those who care for birds and turtles and beaches and ocean life. Give our leaders courage to face the realities of the environmental crisis, and give each one of us wisdom in our retail, transport, and domestic choices, that we may cherish your creation even as we long for its renewal.

* * *

God of passion and compassion, in your Son Jesus you tell us everyone will know we are your disciples if we love one another. Come alongside the employees of this town. Empower all who seek to make this a community that sings to your glory, in great things and in small. Encourage those who struggle at work, in duties, relationships, or expectations, and be close to all who fear for their own future at work or face a time of transition. Inspire those closest to your heart, who do the most ordinary and unheralded tasks in this community, including housekeepers, groundskeepers, maintenance workers, and food service employees. May all their days be praise.

* * *

God of wisdom and understanding, bless all children who find themselves orphans and have few places to turn. Meet us, Lord, in our own loneliness, and make us people who walk with others in their isolation and despair. Through Christ, our living and ascended Lord. Amen.

This is an example of how to introduce major news items without breaking the grounding in scripture or the overall shape of the prayer. The Gulf oil spillage was at the center of public attention for many weeks. Here it is placed in the context of God's promise in Revelation of a new heaven and a new earth. Likewise, again, a cycle of prayer is hidden in the third petition — in this case for all who do less-regarded work around the town — in such a way that it doesn't jar with grander issues earlier in the prayer.

----

(6)

God of justice, your apostle Paul showed us your ways through the cloud of unknowing; be close to any whose life has brought them such a series of setbacks, disappointments, hurts, and failures that they have come to doubt your presence, your purpose, and your power. Make yourself known to those who have been exposed to public humiliation through the media, and family members of any who have become subject to widespread shame. Show your face to all who are unjustly accused, unjustly tried, or unjustly imprisoned. Be close to those who go to work each day dreading what they will have to endure, through cruelty, bullying, or verbal harm; and give strength to those who go home each night fearing what an onslaught of torment or danger may bring. Lord Jesus, make us a people who see justice reshaped by your cross.

* * *

God of the unknown, through your apostle Peter you tell us always to be ready to make our defense to anyone who demands from us an accounting for the hope that is in us; give wisdom to all who work in the criminal justice system. Strengthen the hand of judges, that they may see into people's hearts and know our weakness but also your power to save. Give courage to attorneys, and give heart to those who find themselves a friend to the friendless. Offer patience and discernment to all called to serve as jury members. Lend hope to all who seek to incorporate restorative justice into the life of our communities. Make us, Lord, a people of your justice, but also of your mercy; a people who love you, but also obey your commandments; a people whose sufferings bring you glory, and whose reverence is matched by gentleness.

*   *   *

God of earthquake, wind, fire, and the still small voice, your evangelist John tells us you will give us another Advocate, to be with us forever. Stretch out the hand of your Holy Spirit upon the people of Joplin, Missouri. Comfort the bereaved; embolden the destitute; shelter the homeless. Walk with any today who feel they have no home, no future, no friends, no refuge, no hope, no faith. Continue to be an advocate for the people of Syria, of Jordan, of Egypt, of Bahrain, of Tunisia, and of Libya. Be close to Christians in lands where they are a tiny minority, and be an advocate for those who face persecution and daily fear. Give strength to all who mourn the loss of a loved one in war. Make us, Lord, advocates for your peace. Where we encounter hatred, give us words of love; where we find injury, show us how to pardon; where we meet sadness, help us discover joy.

*   *   *

Hold thou thy cross before our closing eyes; shine through the gloom and point us to the skies. Heaven's morning breaks, and earth's vain shadows hide; in life, in death, O Lord, with us abide. Amen.

Here again the intercession concludes with the verse of a hymn, although in this case the verse has to be gently edited to serve the purpose. (There's no point in rendering public intercessions in the first person singular — the power of intercessions in public worship is that they have the voice of the community behind them.) This is the kind of prayer that seeks to "sweep up" the other scriptural readings when it's clear the preacher intends to engage with only one of them.

ALL SAINTS

Loving Father, your Son said, "Blessed are you poor, but woe to you rich." Be close to all in our city who experience material poverty. Give them friends, give them work, give them hope, give them stability of life. Free them from the fear of crime, of impossible rents, of bad living conditions, of chronic illness. Give us eyes to see the wealth in those we call poor, and the poverty in those we call rich. Speak your words of grace and challenge to all who are materially rich, that they may discover more fully how their wealth may honor and glorify you and make friends in your heavenly mansions.

*　*　*

Merciful Father, your Son said, "Blessed are you hungry, but woe to you who are full." Open your heart to any whose lives are shrouded in hunger. Heal and succor all for whom food becomes the focus of or release from their deepest anxieties, such that eating becomes an escape or a torment. Strengthen all who work in farming and food service industries, and those who seek to cleanse the relationship of humankind to the earth, the seas and the skies, and the living things in each domain. Make all our eating a Eucharistic thanksgiving and a banquet of your hope.

*　*　*

Compassionate Father, your Son said, "Blessed are you who weep, but woe to you who laugh." Spread your arms of mercy around all who grieve. Shelter every parent in this city who's lost a child to sudden, premature, or violent death. Comfort those who feel the economic downturn has taken away their home, their hope, or their identity. And give wisdom and generosity to all for whom life and love and money seem to come easily and painlessly.

*　*　*

Patient Father, your Son said, "Blessed are you who are hated, but woe when all speak well of you." We pray for those we hate. In a mo-

ment of silence we name before you the one we deep down know to be our enemy.... Searching for your grace, we pray for those who hate us. Strengthen the hands of all who strive to bring lingering hatreds to the table of dialogue, in the Middle East, in the Congo, in Sudan, in family therapy, in restorative justice programs. Bring courage to those living in daily fear of military, militia, or terrorist attack. Give your Spirit of truth to all seeking political office, and any who come to distrust others' praise or see the price tag behind others' support.

*   *   *

Holy Father, our rock, our fortress, and our might, when our strife is fierce, our warfare long, steal on our ear the distant triumph song. Make our hearts brave, again, and make our arms strong. Alleluia, Amen.

The Beatitudes are too many in number for a petition to be given over to each one of them: but more or less the same effect is achieved by selecting only a few. The season of All Saints and All Souls is a time when the question of prayer for the dead can get into a tangle; this prayer also followed the death of a student in a university community, and the language in the third petition is carefully framed in circumstances where the cause of death is not yet in the public domain. This kind of petition presupposes that there has been another place in the liturgy to make a more tangible and explicit commemoration: in this case a single rose was brought forward before the opening procession.

SEVEN

Examples: Ordinary Time

(1)

God of compassion, your Son Jesus was brought all who were sick or possessed with demons; visit today all who feel they are in the grip of a power that is not you. Be among, within, and beside those who struggle with addictions to alcohol, gambling, drugs, or damaging forms of sexual expression, and those who live with eating disorders or compulsive conditions. Give strength to your children who are subjected to epileptic attacks or other symptoms that leave them feeling life is out of control and fear is lurking at every corner. Come close to children and parents and partners and friends who find that their loved one's character and mental state is changing slowly before their eyes, and give them grace to find words of truth and moments of trust in which to name the reality of their fear and despair.

*   *   *

God of peace, your Son's disciples hunted for him and said, "Everyone is searching for you"; uphold those who feel they are drowning under the waves of people's expectations, professional responsibilities, or domestic demands. Comfort those who wonder whether they can really do or be or have it all, or any of it, and all who wonder whether they can understand and negotiate and reconcile the yearnings and needs of their hearts and bodies and souls. Be close to any in positions where others look to them for solutions or inspiration or wisdom they fear they do not have. Give us wonder at your design and make us instruments of your peace.

*   *   *

God of love, whose servant Paul said, "I have become all things to all people that by all means I might save some"; we offer to you the issues and situations in our lives that seem beyond our imagination and capacity to resolve. Give hope to those who have illnesses for which there is no cure, remembering all who dwell in houses of hospitality for those who live with HIV/AIDS. Move within international crises that seem to have no end; work among the people of Somalia and Afghanistan, Zimbabwe and Iraq, and all who regard Jerusalem as their home. In a moment of silence we ask you to bring clarity and direction to a part of our life that only you can transform or heal.

*   *   *

God of glory, whose Son Jesus got up before dawn and went out to a deserted place, be with all who are in a deserted place right now. Be near to the ones who feel they are profoundly alone. Speak to those who carry a secret they can share with no one. Bear up all who are walking through the valley of the shadow of death. Cherish your children who are carrying deep wounds, walk with those who cannot see the end of their journey, and embrace any who don't know where to turn, that our restless hearts may find their rest in you, in the power of your Spirit, in union with Christ. Amen.

It is hard to overestimate the pastoral importance of bringing into the center of the church's life and the people's prayers issues that are generally associated with shame. This intercession looks explicitly to draw people into the fellowship of faith who might think of themselves as outside it. The first petition names "those who struggle with addictions to alcohol, gambling, drugs, or damaging forms of sexual expression, and those who live with eating disorders or compulsive conditions" in an explicit attempt to achieve this. The conclusion refers to a familiar prayer, but doesn't quote it: sometimes it's best to make a gesture, and let the congregation do the rest for themselves.

(2)

Transfiguring God, you spoke from the cloud and called Jesus your beloved child. Bless those who struggle in love, any who don't know how best to love a child, or how best to love a parent. Be with grandparents who wrestle with how to show their love to a grandchild when families have moved far away or have split up and face-to-face contact is very limited. Speak words of comfort to any who have never known what it means to be truly beloved, and those for whom love has always been tangled up with emotional or physical traps. Bless all for whom home is a place not of safety but of fear and horror and lament. Hold us in your everlasting arms today, that we may know we are your beloved children, your heart's desire.

✳ ✳ ✳

Transforming God, your servant Elisha said to Elijah, "I will not leave you." Be with those who are alone. Be close to all who grieve the loss of a spouse, the end of a marriage, the lack of a partner, or the loneliness of being unheard, unnoticed, or never understood. Send your Holy Spirit upon all who are in prison, and upon prisoners of conscience. Meet us, Lord, in our solitude, be with us in our despair, and help us find you in one another.

✳ ✳ ✳

Tender God, your Son Jesus talked with Moses and Elijah. Strengthen all who work in the legal profession, and those who create, administer, and enforce the law of the land. Embolden those who are prophets, who display your ways and your purposes in times and places where people have strayed far from your truth. Give us grace to know when it is the time for law and when it is the time for prophecy, when for careful planning and when for spontaneity, when for disciplined obedience and when for joyful risk-taking. Surround us with those who will tell us the truth, and open our hearts to receive wisdom from the angels you send to us.

✳ ✳ ✳

*Truthful God, your Son's transfiguration was more than his compan-
ions could comprehend. Open our hearts to your peace which passes
all understanding. Open our eyes to see the transfiguration you bring.
In a moment of quiet we ask for your inspiration in a place in our
lives in need of your transfiguration. . . . Strengthen those who inspire
us, with words, with music, with example, with courage, with faithfulness, with hope. Make us, Lord, a people who inspire others, that
many may find in us a community of your transfiguration, companions in conversation with your Son, our savior, Jesus Christ. Amen.*

As noted earlier, transfiguration, along with incarnation and resurrection, is
one of the three principal forms of intercession — and perhaps the most
neglected. Here is a prayer on the last Sunday before Lent, when the story of
the Transfiguration is often read. The balance of Moses and Elijah is a gift to
the intercessor, looking to balance themes of law and prophecy.

(3)

*God of heaven and earth, your people brought to Aaron all their gold
for him to make a golden calf of worship. We come to you today in
bewilderment of the gold we have worshiped in the financial markets.
If we have been idolaters, show us how and where we must repent.
Where your people are losing livelihoods and savings and homes and
hope, be among them with your peace which surpasses all understanding. If our economy has been founded on the sand of foolishness
and reckless assumption, show us where the rock of sustainable
finance lies. Where politicians and executives and bankers and
householders are scurrying frantically for rescue packages, be among
them with truth and honor and justice and the power of your Holy
Spirit. As the king in the parable instructed his servants to go out into
the main streets and invite all whom they found, both good and bad,
empower us to be among the people on Main Street with invitations
to your banquet and the gentleness of your peace.*

* * *

God of life and love, in your Son Jesus, you speak of heaven as a wedding banquet. Bless those who like Jesus are single. Be with all who long to know the love of a partner and the opportunity to nurture children and those who find the freedom of singleness to be more of a burden or a cause for grief. Send your Spirit on any who are single again: those who mourn the person that used to share their heart and any for whom the death of a marriage has brought bitterness and deep wounds. Nurture all preparing for marriage and those newly married, that they may meet you in their longing to know one another and the crafting of lifelong habits of intimacy; all whose passion for their partner and the dream of their life together seems lost in the cares and urgency and responsibilities of work and home; those for whom having children has brought heartbreak as much as joy; all looking to discover what life and love mean when children are far away. Be close to those who don't know if their love is something you or your church allows or understands.

* * *

God of justice and mercy, your servant Moses pleaded with you to remember your servants and you changed your mind about punishing your people. We recognize before you the things that make us burn with anger. Give us grace to find good ways to let our anger energize our ministry, our compassion, and our witness. But give us also malleable hearts, that we may be able to change our minds and recognize when we have been too hasty, too ignorant, or too self-righteous. Give grace to those for whom acknowledging their mistake or foolishness is too humiliating or too risky or too public. Bless ministries of reconciliation between offender and victim, employer and employee, developing states and wealthy ones, and between nations at war. Make us, Lord, a merciful people whose hearts and minds are shaped like yours, empowered by your forgiveness and inspired by your promise of everlasting life. In Christ's name. Amen.

This prayer was offered in October 2008, just as the global crash was in its greatest intensity. The first petition strives to blend a mood of penitence with one of dismay, while trying to remain intercession rather than turning into an act of confession. The second petition goes through a diverse range of social contexts in relation to marriage: the final phrase is one that is designed to include without making judgment, drawing undue attention to itself, or risking wording that some present could not say "Amen" to.

———

(4)

God of judgment, in Jesus you remind us that we know not the day nor the hour of your coming; make us bridesmaids for the marriage of heaven and earth. Fill our lamps with oil of gladness, of compassion, of kindness, of perseverance, of faithfulness, and of patience. Look upon those who long for your coming, who cry out "How long, O Lord, how long?" Be close to those in prison of body, mind, or spirit; any for whom a close relationship is a daily dance with despair; all in relentless physical pain; and those living in oppressive political circumstances, in Zimbabwe, Sudan, Burma, and Tibet. Give hope to all who feel they are always the bridesmaid: left behind in their career, or in love, or in financial circumstances; and meet us in our own anxiety that the party is really going on somewhere else. Heal our envy and jealousy, Lord, and empower us to enjoy the place where you have set us; make our light shine so brightly that it may light the path of your Son when he comes in glory.

* * *

God of gentleness, in the broken body of your Son we see your love for those who live with physical, sensory, intellectual, or emotional disability. Be close to those whose impairment dominates their view or perception of the world, and any whose impairment seems to dominate or impair the world's view of them. Inspire all communities where those with developmental disabilities share their lives with those without them. Bless all who strive for equality under the law and equality of perception for those who do not wish their disability to be the most obvious or interesting thing about their lives. Give grace to any who hum-

bly long to discover and practice better ways to cherish and be present to those whose differences they find troubling. And show us each the ways in which we ourselves are disabled, even if those are ways we keep hidden from others, that we may come to you as broken people resting only on one another's shoulders and on your Son's nail-scarred hands.

* * *

God of wonder and mystery, whose Son died at the hands of politicians and yet now presides in the council of heaven; inspire this nation's leaders, and give them the spirit of wisdom and understanding, of council and inward strength, of knowledge and true fear of you. Be close to all who live with political disappointment; as so many in the electoral process so explicitly name their differences, help them to rediscover those deeper things they share, that the economic, diplomatic, ecological, and political tasks of government may be ones that honor your way and make this nation a blessing to your world. In a moment of silence we lay before you our deepest hopes and fears for our political leaders.

* * *

God of the living and the dead, through your servant Paul you promise not to let us be uninformed about those who have died. We recognize before you our own fragility and mortality. Bless all who are sick, and those who are close to death. We place upon your altar any whose names are written on our hearts and on yours, whose lives shaped our lives and whose deaths characterize our notion of death. Finally, Lord, we name before you those whose deaths we cannot contemplate because their lives are dearer to us than our own; may their lives draw us closer to your life, and their love closer to your love. In Christ's name. Amen.

It's important both to name disability as an important issue in epic and lyric experience, and to ensure that "the disabled" don't become a "them" that the congregation looks at with pity from afar. The second petition seeks to do this by being the second petition, rather than the first, by beginning with the brokenness of God, and by exploring the diversity of contexts the umbrella term covers. The intercession doesn't end with an obvious collect or hymn quotation: it's best not to get too predictable.

———

(5)

Transforming God, in Jesus you set us free from crippling burdens. Walk today with all who are crippled — by regrets about the past, by debt, sickness, or disability in the present, by fears for the future. In a moment of silence we name before you one person whose life is crippled by bitterness or anxiety . . . As you offer the Sabbath as a gift, give grace to those who find they cannot rest, and all whose peace in you is inhibited by duty or distraction or distress or despair. Make us, Lord, a Sabbath to one another, that as you unravel our crippled hearts you may make us a people among whom others may find your rest.

* * *

Tender God, you adore us like a parent, yet make yourself as vulnerable to us as a child. Give grace to all families who face the beginning of the academic year with trepidation. Bless those who find it bewildering to let go, or feel bereft of companionship or purpose when a bedroom and a place at table are suddenly empty. Guide the words and gestures of all who are present to us in our struggles. Empower and renew all hospital, college, military, and prison chaplains, and be close to those they serve. Come to us, Lord, and abide with us in our times of loneliness and abandonment.

* * *

Consuming God, you have made yourself known in tempest, trumpet, and terror, but you invite us to gather with you in the city of joy. Visit the people of Pakistan as they endure trembling and flood and fear. Look with favor on that country, besieged by extremism and instability and acrimony, and restore it in your sight as a place of hope and growth and harmony. Send your Spirit upon Christians in Pakistan, that they may flourish in faith amid threats of persecution. Through this communion at your table, Lord, make us one with your suffering and persecuted people, that they may find solace in us, as we find strength in you.

* * *

Teach us, good Lord, to serve thee as thou deservest; to give and not to count the cost; to fight and not to heed the wounds; to labor and not to ask for any reward, save that of knowing that we do thy will. Through Jesus Christ our Lord, Amen.

This intercession ends with a well-known medieval prayer. If such prayers are not introduced into the liturgy, it's possible that some members of the congregation could miss out on them altogether. The first petition tries to steer a path between acknowledging the scriptural context — of the healing of a crippled man — and recognizing that today it's important not to see disability in wholly, or even primarily, negative terms, but to acknowledge the disability of perception, in the eye of the beholder, also.

(6)

Holy God, in Christ you wholly abandoned yourself to us. Embrace those who feel wholly abandoned. Be close to all who walk the long road of instability in mental well-being, and bless those who find it hard to sustain relationships of permanence and trust. Be our companion when we feel abandoned in grief, when we yearn for words of comfort but find them hard to hear. Speak to the hearts of all who feel abandoned in faith and a long way from your intimate touch. Bring succor to those who are in physical pain and know it is only going to get worse. In a moment of silence we bring to you one person we know who feels abandoned by you. . . . Give us grace to abandon ourselves to you, in the secret places of our hearts.

* * *

Beckoning God, in Jesus you called the rich young man to enter your Father's kingdom. When you call us to go, give us courage to travel, to risk, to change. When you call us to sell, fill us with joy as you make our lives simpler that other may simply live. When you call us to give, bring us friends we never knew we could make and wise guides we never thought we could meet. When you call us to come, keep us faithful to your commandments, and set us on fire with love for you. And when you call us to follow, instill us with humility to accept the guidance of others and the patience to walk in step with you.

* * *

Wondrous God, in Jesus we discover that nothing is impossible with you. Encourage all who face mountainous debts, and give hope to those for whom mortgage payments are an unbearable burden. Bless organizations in our city that provide capital for first-time homeowners and small businesses, and prosper the work of those building a new future. Shelter any who know they have done something terribly wrong, and can't face the pain of those they have scarred and wounded or the shame of showing their face in public. Cherish all whose dreams have been shattered, and uphold their tender hearts that they may learn to dream again.

* * *

Be with us, Lord, in grief, in despair, in temptation, in pain, and in fear, and give us strength whate'er betide us, to bear us through the evil days, that even when the clouds gather above us and the earth shake beneath us, we can look to the wounded hands of your Son and the sustaining grace of your Holy Spirit, and say, It is well, it is well with my soul. Amen.

Sometimes a person comes to church having no words to say for how awful his or her life feels at that moment. From time to time it can be helpful to switch the default mode of worship from thankfulness and celebration to lament and compassion. A prayer like "Bring succor to those who are in physical pain and know it is only going to get worse" is very different from a conventional prayer for healing, but it may do more justice to where a person is in life and faith. The five instructions to the rich young man — go, sell, give, come, follow — could have shaped five petitions; but the pastoral need to acknowledge pain was too great on this occasion, and they were folded into a single petition instead.

———————

(7)

God of love, you have taught us through your servant Paul that love bears all things, believes all things, hopes all things, endures all things. Be with those who have much to endure. Strengthen the people of Haiti: the homeless, the bereaved, the bewildered, the sick, the starving. As your people cry out to you for hope, healing, and help, give them food, give them faith, give them friends. As we see the crumbling foundations of many homes, show us where the foundations of our own lives are fragile, and give us wisdom to strengthen those foundations before disaster comes to us.

✳ ✳ ✳

God of grace, you have shown us that love rejoices in the truth; that love is not envious or boastful or arrogant or resentful, and does not insist on its own way. Empower those in our city who are wealthy, that they may find institutions in which to invest their money so that they and the whole community may benefit from your blessing and desire for our well-being. Speak to all for whom the truth is hard to see, who fear to back down for fear of being trodden on, or who want to be firm in the face of bullying. Give courage to any who grieve that their talents are going to waste or feel that their future has become bleak due to unemployment or discrimination or disappointment. Heal those who carry wounds of bitterness for years and decades, and surround us with those who can make us laugh at ourselves.

✳ ✳ ✳

God of hope, you promise us that love never ends. Restore all for whom love has ended. Walk with any who try to sustain relationships where passion or trust or tenderness has died. Sustain those who have tried so hard for so long but now feel they can go on no longer. And be among your children whose hearts beat for those they love but see no longer, those who have had to bury their own children, all who try to live again after a partner has died, or who face the future without a parent or friend or mentor who had always been there for them.

✳   ✳   ✳

Lord, you have taught us that all our doings without love are nothing worth: send your Holy Spirit and pour into our hearts that most excellent gift of love, the true bond of peace and of all virtues, without which whoever lives is counted dead before you. Grant this for your only Son Jesus Christ's sake. Amen.

This intercession concludes with a regular collect: sometimes there's nothing better than the time-honed language found in a prayer book. The prayer as a whole is based on 1 Corinthians 13, and seeks to infuse the familiar language with a range of human experience and concern. Sometimes it's possible for one short passage of scripture to carry a whole intercessory prayer in this way — so long as one lets go of any idea that one can exhaust the meaning of the text.

---

(8)

God of new life, there's a wideness in your mercy like the wideness of the sea. Be close today to all who know what it means to be a prodigal. Your love is broader than the measure of our mind. Have mercy on those who find themselves in the pigsty out of foolishness or hastiness or greed or willfulness. Your heart is most wonderfully kind. Breathe life into the pigsties of your world, and because in Jesus you came into the pigsty of our estrangement from you and brought us home, send us into places of shame and humiliation and despair, that we may find you there and find ourselves in your service.

* * *

God of mercy, with healing balm our souls are filled and every faithless murmur stilled. Be close today to all who know what it means to be the one who is bitter and resentful. As with a mother's tender hand you gently lead us, heal all who look on the joy and forgiveness of others with hurt and anger and hardness of heart. Bless all in our city who are elderly, and any who find their later years are dogged by frustration and loneliness and regret. Cleanse and soften the spirits of any who cannot accept a stranger's presence, react with hostility to the naming of old wounds, or will not tolerate another's happiness. Make us a people who are a blessing to others and find joy in one another's joy.

* * *

God of restoration, you have promised good to us; you will our shield and portion be as long as life endures. Send and encourage ambassadors of reconciliation in the Holy Land, in Pakistan, in Afghanistan, in Iraq, in Sudan, and in the Congo. You have reconciled the world to yourself; give us hope that we may be reconciled to those who have hurt us or whom we have hurt, and give us the will to take gentle yet bold steps to offer grace where relationships have become tangled, confused, or poisoned. Strengthen all who teach languages and work in translation and cross-cultural communication. Teach us to speak other languages, and help us learn to speak yours.

* * *

In a moment of silence we offer those cries of anguish and hope that come from so deep in our hearts we have no words to express them. . . . O Love that wilt not let us go, we rest our weary soul in thee; we give thee back the life we owe, that in thine ocean depths its flow may richer, fuller be. Amen.

Hymns can be used with the same diversity of purpose as scriptural texts. Here three hymns — "There's a Wideness in God's Mercy," "Amazing Grace," and "O Love That Wilt Not Let Me Go" — are interwoven and more or less fill the space a scriptural text would usually take. But there are plenty of more conventional references too — for example, "you have reconciled the world to yourself," and the language that refers to the parable of the prodigal son.

(9)

Holy God, your Son lost his life that we might find ours; be close to those who are losing their life today. Where your children are near to death, fill their aching hearts with hope, their grieving families with love, and their final moments with grace. Where your children are throwing their futures away, through reckless living, cycles of addiction, or lunges of despair, bring them new patience, deeper hope, and courageous friends. And where your children are facing acutely the cost of discipleship, the sacrifice of faithfulness, or the fear that their labors have been in vain, give them a double portion of your Spirit.

* * *

Nurturing God, whose life was made fully known in a manger in Bethlehem; shine your star above the homes of our city where there are newborn babies. Bring the wonder of new life to those who are tired at heart; give strength to all for whom the relentlessness, the intensity, and the expense of parenthood is an unbearable strain on their energy, their finances, or their closest relationships; and give wisdom and understanding to grandparents and friends and professional caregivers, and all who feel love, concern, and confusion but hesitate to interfere.

* * *

Truthful God, in whose fear is the beginning of wisdom; we recall before you those who have been our teachers; all who have urged and inspired us, and cheered us on our way; who taught us to read, and to read your Word; to count, and to count your blessings; to walk, and to walk in your ways; to sing, and to sing your praises; bless those who are our teachers today, who see the possibility in us and bring out the best in us and give us goals to reach for and examples to follow; and make us teachers ourselves, that in seeking to shape others in your faith, we may find ourselves face to face with you. Amen.

One of the most poignant forms of powerlessness in Western society today is the grandparent who, after the break-up of a family, doesn't know how best to exercise their rights and responsibilities. Most congregations will include such people. The second petition alludes to such a plight. The final collect seeks to draw together many of the blessings of life in an educational setting.

(10)

Covenanting God, your people betrayed you and exchanged their liberation for an idol. Be close to all who experience profound betrayal; who know what it means to trust and be let down, to promise and be forgotten, to sacrifice and be ignored, to believe and be heartbroken. Bless all who struggle with anger, bitterness, and thoughts of revenge, and those who wonder if they can ever trust again. And yet you changed your mind and did not visit disaster on your people. Fill the hearts of all who are searching for the grace to change their minds, to try again, to hope, to live beyond resentment, and to trust their own judgment. Give us grace to change our own minds, to overcome our pride and hard-heartedness, and to enter the freedom you promise us.

* * *

Liberating God, empower all your children who long for the freedom to vote, to live without fear, to break out from oppression, to remake

119

their societies as equals under the law. Sustain those in Libya who seek a new way of life. Bless the people of Yemen and of Syria as they hope for a peaceful transition of power. Visit your people in Zimbabwe, Burma, and lands where violence is part of government control and opposition incurs danger. Strengthen those who work for a healthy future for Iraq and Afghanistan. And encourage all who experience life in this country as one of disadvantage, fear, or slavery.

* * *

Loving God, you walk with us in the valley, accompany us in the wilderness, speak with us on the mountain, and promise us flourishing life with you. Be present to all who face serious illness. Give them hope, alleviate their pain, help them to plan their future, and above all bring them friends. Bless the work of hospital chaplains and all who listen and enter the mystery of pain with the sick and the dying. In a moment of quiet we offer you one person we know to be facing the reality of the end of life. . . . With healing balm their soul fill and every faithless murmur still.

* * *

Transforming God, you turn our weakness into your opportunity, our sin into your grace, our pride into your wisdom, our folly into your mercy, our evil into your grace. Turn the wounds of our sin into the glory of your resurrected body, that we might live more truly, love more deeply, and follow more faithfully, now and forever. Amen.

Where and when do people change their mind? Without a change of mind and heart, reconciliation and wisdom are impossible. But where does that transformation take place? Should it not be the aspiration of the intercessor that in this moment of full engagement, focused on pleading with God to change the world, members of the congregation might be in a perfect condition to accept a change in themselves? The first petition here sets such transformation in the context of the covenantal story — and the concluding collect sets it in the context of God's overarching grace.

(11)

Take our lives, and let them be consecrated, Lord, to thee. As you made your Son Jesus Christ your talent to trade in the marketplace of your creation, take our lives and trade with us in the marketplace of your kingdom. Look with favor on your servants who trade today, in the places of wealth and power, in the intensity of spice and rice exchanges in the two-thirds world, in suburban malls and rural market towns. Take our hands, and let them move at the impulse of thy love. Bless all who use their hands to craft products for sale, and any who face daily risk of injury and disfigurement through working with dangerous equipment. Empower all who use their hands to nurture and heal our bodies: pour your spirit on our hospitals and all who offer care through them and who look to them for hope in times of distress, fear, and pain. In a moment of silence we offer you one person we know to be looking in dismay through the veil of an uncertain medical future.

✳   ✳   ✳

Take our lips, and let them be filled with messages from thee. Speak into the hearts of all who put their names forward in public elections. Bring strength and encouragement to those who are seeking to make true democracy a reality in our neighborhoods and communities. Bless those who are trying to forge democracy in Libya, Syria, Tunisia, and Iraq. Give hope to the people of Greece and Italy and to all who are terrified in the face of the financial fragility of the global economy. Take our moments and our days; let them flow in ceaseless praise. As you encourage us to use our talents, show us ways in which we can take steps to release people from slavery and make all your world in every corner sing with the joy of abundant life.

✳   ✳   ✳

Take our intellects, and use every power as thou shalt choose. Bless all who study as they bring faith and intellect into harmony, and make a symphony of head, hand, and heart in responding to your call. Strengthen university chaplaincies and make them fruitful in helping students find you in one another, find one another in you, and find your kingdom in mission, study, and friendship. Take our feet, and let them be swift and beautiful for thee. Give us, Lord, good work to do. When we doubt or despair, give us friends to remind us where we are going. When we hurt or fail, give us your grace to try again. And when we are frail and lost, meet us in your Son and bring us home.

* * *

Take our wills, and make them yours; they shall be no longer ours. Take our hearts, they are thine own; they shall be thy royal throne. Take our loves, our Lord, we pour at thy feet their treasure store. Take ourselves, and we shall be ever, only, all for thee. Amen.

Here again is an intercession shaped entirely around one text — in this case, the hymn "Take My Life, and Let It Be" — translated into a first person plural context. This prayer is intended for a service of commissioning and commitment, where those stepping forward for a new ministry are encouraged to understand that ministry in the light of the needs and hopes of the whole church.

(12)

Lord God, fount of every blessing, you accompanied your chosen people in the wilderness and lived with their forgetfulness and impatience. Walk with all who inhabit the wilderness today. Cast your hand of mercy on the people of Syria. Give hope to all who love Afghanistan. Be among everyone who believed that in the Arab Spring they were leaving slavery but today find themselves not in the promised land but in the desert. Give courage to the people of Greece and all who face austerity measures that are stripping them of the life they hold dear. Move in the hearts of students who are finding their college years a wilderness, and of all who feel lonely, discouraged, or close to despair. In a moment of silence we bring to you one person we know to be in the wilderness today. . . .

* * *

Never-ceasing stream of mercy, be a guiding star to all for whom touch and intimacy are matters of fear, pain, and shame. Bless the work of college sexual assault support services. Work in the lives of those for whom sex is a form of manipulation, exploitation, and cruelty. Be close to all who experience sex as a matter of pathology, addiction, secrecy, deceit, or regret. Heal each one of us in our places of hurt, hunger, and rejection.

* * *

God of grace, you have brought us safe thus far, and you will lead us home. Help us to face the truth about our past. Give wisdom to all who find they and their family have made their living in ways that now make them feel ashamed. Give patience to those who seek repentance, or reparation, or restoration from those they believe have hurt them or their ancestors or their people. Open our hearts to the ways we participate in structures of oppression and subjugation. Give each one of us humility and faith to cry out to you for mercy, and perseverance to walk the slow journey to integrity and responsibility. Surround us with friends who will tell us who we are and what we have done, and who will love us even when they know the truth about us. Show us who it is with whom we must be reconciled before you will heal us.

* * *

God of mercy, you took the poison of our sin and mixed it with the blood of your Son to make the fount of your grace. Pour upon us the abundance of your love that we might be lifted up as signs to all your people of what your love can do. In Christ's name. Amen.

There's no contradiction between epic and lyric frames of reference. This prayer makes more explicit than usual the epic scale of the forces at work that weigh people down: "Open our hearts to the ways we participate in structures of oppression and subjugation" — but in a way that does not allow the congregation to assume all the evil lies far and away. But at the same time a lyric turn makes the prayer personal and moving — "Heal each one of us in our places of hurt, hunger, and rejection." It's the appropriate combination and confluence of the two that produces the right effect. Words from "Come, Thou Fount of Every Blessing" and "Amazing Grace" offer additional lyric texture.

---

(13)

Holy God, whose steadfast love is our eternal song, fill us, your church, with praises that never end. Make our life together the place we make a melody as your people that we could never sing alone. Embrace and uphold all who long to join this chorus of grace and wonder if there is a place for them in it. Embolden and inspire those who find your eternal song stirring them to a new or deepening place of faith. Give us grace to join our voices to one another. Show us your face in the face of those with whom we have disagreements. Pour your Spirit of counsel and wisdom upon the places in your church where the melody of faith is obscured by discord. When we lose our way, retune our hearts to you and surround us with the song of your saints.

*   *   *

Son of God, who is for us the living bread that came down from heaven, draw us to you through the grace of our daily needs. Make our daily need for food and drink deepen our hunger for you, whose body is true food and whose blood is true drink. In a moment of silence we name before you one place we hunger for your true presence. . . . By your Spirit, make our hunger the place we know your truth. Keep us hungry for your presence in our midst. Give us hearts to see the needs of one another: for loving care, for food and shelter, and for gentle compassion. Teach us tenderness when we need others to help with our own daily needs. Bless parents of incoming first year students as their daily relationship with their children changes in a new stage of life. Through your grace, make our everyday needs an occasion to live into your mercy anew every morning.

✳   ✳   ✳

Holy Spirit, who stirs within us beyond what we can see or know or comprehend, lead us into true life. Help us to trust our lives to you more deeply and show us what true life is. Encourage police officers and others who daily encounter difficult situations through their responsibility to safeguard neighborhoods throughout this city. Inspire men and women who work to strengthen communities in ways that inspire trust in each of the five districts of the city. Pour your grace upon all who seek to listen with compassion to someone else's struggle. Visit places throughout our world where trust is eroded, where relationships between neighbors are places of suspicion rather than mutual confidence. In the power of the risen Christ, take away from us those things which we do not need so that we may have space to receive what you want to give us. Awaken us to your stirring in our neighborhoods and communities, and match that to your stirring within our hearts so that we may find our place in your kingdom this very day.

✳   ✳   ✳

All these prayers we ask in the name of our Lord Jesus Christ, who with the Father and the Holy Spirit lives and reigns forever. Amen.

Naming police officers draws out a larger issue for prayer — trust within communities. This is one way of dealing with a topic suggested by a prayer cycle: making more of it instead of less, seeing it as a gift rather than as a burden to incorporate.

(14)

Lord Jesus, who spoke to your disciples in the storm, speak your words over us today. Speak to our lives your words of hope, "Take heart, I am here, do not be afraid." Speak your words over places of sickness, over those in the hospital, and any recovering from surgery [name]. Speak to our places of quiet and hidden suffering, and our griefs that are deeper than words. Speak to our places of fear, "Take heart, I am here, do not be afraid." Speak your words over the places in our world where fear feeds hatred. Speak your words over the places where fear creates enemies, "Take heart, I am here, do not be afraid." Help us to live in the power that is stronger than fear, the strength of the Holy Spirit.

Lord Jesus, who asked Peter to walk towards you on the water, encourage all who walk towards you in faith today. When we long to see miracles, help us to live in ways that require trust and faith. Be with the many of us who are returning from mission trips and camps, where we have discovered you anew in places where we found you hungry or thirsty, places where you needed shelter or friendship, places where you were sick or wounded. Inspire us as we return to our daily lives to walk in ways that deepen the closeness we found with you in [name of place] and in our own city's poorest areas. Help us to do things that require faith in your resurrection and that rest upon the gifts of your Holy Spirit. Help us to find our place in your living body called the church.

Lord Jesus, who came to the small boat tossed by waves, move toward the places where your people are battered and bruised. Be with the people of Somalia who are engulfed in a wave of famine, with all who are working to bring relief from within and outside the country, and all who are engulfed by watching the suffering of their loved ones without food. Be with all who seek refuge of any kind, and all who are present to the struggles of others. Give wisdom to your church around the world; give strength in the places where your church is tossed by waves. Call us to you when our differences and disputes threaten the unity of our one baptism. Call us to you despite our weakness and failures. Inspire us, like you, to move toward those who are tossed in the waves; empower us to move toward the battered and the storm-tossed in the ever-trusting love of the Holy Spirit.

All these prayers we ask in the name of our living Lord who with the Father and Spirit is glorified forever. Amen.

This prayer inhabits the story of Jesus and the disciples on the storm-tossed boat. It is unified by this one theme which invites the congregation to enter imaginatively into the scripture for the day in a mode of prayer. It is like meditation with a single focus; but importantly, it is the language of prayer rather than sermon.

———————

(15)

Christ our Lord, who came not to be served but to serve, lead your children into the service that is perfect freedom. As you gave yourself for us, show us the freedom found in seeking one another's flourishing. Come near to those who serve with singleness of heart in everyday ways in the ordinary places where they are and all for whom leadership means daily presence, humble devotion, and quiet courage. Send your Spirit upon the many who carry positions of leadership on this campus or the responsibility of leadership on national and international concerns that affect the well-being of multitudes. Open our eyes to see in every opportunity for responsibility an occasion to serve others as though serving you, full of tenderness and mercy and compassion.

* * *

God who shaped every wonder of creation, make your joy known in the height and breadth and depth of all you have made. Hear us when we exclaim with praise and draw near to us when we cry, for you know our every sorrow and yet rejoice in us. In a moment of silence, we entrust to your embrace one person whose sorrow is in our hearts this day. . . . In times of bearing one another's cares, make your mercies known here and now, near and far, today and always. Pour your love into the lives of children who need a nurturing home. Welcome into your arms boys and girls who long for a place to call their home. Bless foster parents and adoptive parents who offer a place for them to belong. As you rejoice in us and call us your own, shape our hearts to be like yours, to celebrate the height and breadth and depth of one another's joy and, most of all, to rejoice in the things that bring joy to you.

* * *

Risen Lord, who gave your life as ransom for many, renew the life of your church through places of resurrection hope. Send your Spirit upon your church in places where such hope seems far away. Have compassion upon all who have servanthood pressed upon them and any who are bound against their will. Wrap your sustaining and fearless love around those whose lives have been taken from them through economic hardship or fear of physical harm. By your Spirit, steady us and give us courage in the places we are most in need of your grace. Through your mercy, make us bearers of Christ's redeeming love.

* * *

All these prayers we ask in the name of Christ our Lord who with the Father and the Spirit lives and reigns forever. Amen.

Naming oppressive realities with indirect language opens the prayer wider rather than narrowing it — that is, "all who have servanthood pressed upon them," "any who are bound against their will," and "those whose lives have been taken from them." These phrases capture everything from sex trafficking to child soldiers to forced labor in a way that respects the lives of those affected rather than making the prayer about an issue. It is very difficult to pray satisfactorily about issues; rather, it is best to pray for people.

(16)

Forgiving God, who in Jesus makes possible new beginnings, show your renewing hope in the midst of new beginnings here today. Bless the teachers who have been led to share their gifts in this new year of Sunday School. Give them your inspiration and wisdom as they nurture the faith of children and grow together with them. Stir the hearts of boys and girls discovering the wonders of your love. Bless the third graders who have received Bibles today. Speak to them as they read and study and learn to live the story of redeeming love found in its pages. Show each one of us the power of the new life you make possible through Jesus. Send your Holy Spirit into the places we await new beginnings. Draw near to us in the places we seek your forgiveness. Strengthen us when we need to find grace to forgive a brother or sister.

✳   ✳   ✳

O God our help in ages past and our hope for years to come, comfort us as we remember the fear and shock we felt a decade ago. Take into your heart the men, women, and children whose lives were lost in New York, Washington, and Pennsylvania; comfort and heal their families and loved ones. We grieve for the violence that has followed since that day. Come close to all those who mourn and have not stopped mourning. Give hope to Americans serving in places of war, and to their families. Be with the people of Iraq and Afghanistan, and all who face daily danger. Strengthen us to seek peace and pursue it, and show us how to heal wounds rather than inflict them. Pour your grace upon relationships between people of different faiths in this country, and unite us in the places we share common concern for the poor through actions of justice and mercy. Give to the President and all leaders understanding and compassion as they seek to live into the highest ideals of America.

✳   ✳   ✳

Steadfast God, who led your people to freedom by your constant presence in fire and cloud, keep watch over your church by day and by night. Abide with those among our congregation who are recovering from surgery and give them strength for each day: [names]. Enfold with your tender love the family of [name] as they grieve his death. Come close to all of us as we remember [name]'s life, and strengthen us to remember the many ways we saw Jesus in him. In a moment of silence we bring before you now someone who needs your watch-keeping love. . . . Through your Holy Spirit, bless and keep each and every one of your children through the hours of the day and in all the watches of the night.

* * *

All these prayers we ask in the name of Jesus Christ who with the Father and the Holy Spirit lives and reigns forever. Amen.

Occasionally during Ordinary Time, a day of national significance arises in a way that needs to be addressed directly in the prayers. This prayer was written for the tenth anniversary of the September 11, 2001, terrorist attacks (the anniversary fell on a Sunday in 2011). The challenge in praying on the anniversary of a tragedy is to pray specifically enough to show deep remembering but not so specifically that the tragedy is re-created for listeners. This prayer allots space to lament for the unhealed wounds ten years hence. Lament is sometimes the only imaginable place to begin intercessions. Specifying the wide range of people whose lives have been impacted by 9/11 widens the prayer beyond American concerns to include people of other nations affected. It also purposely widens the congregation's imagination in prayer to include people of other faiths and asks God for some specific help in healing. The language of the prayer is such that no one affected in any way by this tragedy is beyond the reach of God's love. It purposely avoids taking sides or placing blame or drawing lines.

In the congregation where this was prayed, a patriarch of the congregation had died in the preceding week after a long period of suffering, and so the pastoral prayer that Sunday needed to encompass the shared grief of his death as well. As is often the case in a local church, there are causes for joy and sorrow interlaced through everything, and this prayer seeks to capture that reality.

(17)

Holy God, whose risen Son shows your power made perfect in weakness, make us people who live from grace to grace in the power of your Spirit. Dwell in us today and make us people who dwell in you this very moment. God of glory, who knows our every weakness and the ways weakness makes us fearful, deepen our trust in your perfect love. We bring before you in a time of silence one place of our own weakness in body or in mind or in spirit, a place you are inviting us to trust your unfailing power. . . . By your Spirit, transform fear into faith. Beckon us through our places of weakness, and bring us to your everlasting glory.

*   *   *

God of daily bread, whose Son told his followers to take nothing for their journey except sandals and a walking staff, set our feet in the direction of your kingdom. Mark the path of your church by our pilgrim feet. Help us to discover the beauty of the simple sandals and walking staff you have given us. Set our hearts to discover the riches of your kingdom. Teach us to walk two by two as brothers and sisters in faith and so to find our true life in you. Sustain us that we may sustain one another. Nourish our most basic needs of daily bread that we may nourish one another. Walk by our side when we carry a loved one through a difficult time. Through your Spirit present to us in one another, strengthen us in faith, confirm us in hope, and perfect us in love.

*   *   *

God of all nations, whose good news spreads to the ends of the earth and the ends of time, make us instruments of your peace. We bring before you this nation and all who live in it. As Americans celebrate freedom and unity this weekend, guide and direct this nation as we seek yet a more perfect union. Help us to discover true freedom which benefits all who live here, not only a few. Make this land be a place where the goodness of life, the blessing of well-being, and the bounty

131

of community can be found in abundance for all. Give your wisdom to those who lead this nation. By your Spirit, give us patience to seek the paths that make for peace in this city, this nation, and around your world. Give wisdom to the leaders and people of Iraq in these days of new beginning. Comfort people whose fear of unrest and ongoing fighting makes them captives in their homes; send your Holy Spirit on the nations of Iran, Afghanistan, and Sudan. Help us, your church, to be a healing balm in the midst of injury and hatred, in this country and throughout the earth.

✳   ✳   ✳

All these prayers we ask in the name of our Lord Jesus Christ, who with the Father and Spirit lives and reigns forever.

Independence Day always falls during Ordinary Time as a day of national significance. Addressing this in prayer can be a way to name some of the ways America has fallen short of its ideals while also celebrating the dreams planted deep in the American imagination. Toward this end, this prayer uses recognizable historic rhetoric such as "a more perfect union," and it draws upon the political language of freedom and unity. The prayer specifically seeks to avoid self-laudatory, self-congratulatory language ("God bless America") but rather stirs up a sense that Americans have much yet to seek and to do. Interspersing language that is historic and political in tone with the language of scripture widens the prayer, preventing it from falling into expected nationalistic platitudes. Choosing words with multiple layers of meaning, both in scripture and in public life, serves to widen the scope of concerns. On this day, when is so important to pray for the nation and its leaders, often intercessors find it difficult to know what to ask for without sounding partisan. Here is an example of drawing upon the language of scripture to know what we might dare ask of God for the nation ("Give us patience to seek the paths that make for peace") and for the church ("Help us to be a healing balm").

EIGHT

Examples: Occasions

The person who has learned to offer prayers of intercession in the regular rhythm of weekly congregational worship should be well prepared to offer prayers in the more challenging setting of crisis, tragedy, mixed-faith, or ad hoc gatherings. The following prayers were all offered in contexts where those present were of all faiths and none, and where the right to speak of God, let alone to God on others' behalf, had to be earned by visible sensitivity, respect, and understanding.

Such settings don't always bring out the best in Christian intercessors. Some find it hard to change gear from a habitual worship setting, and fall into the language of "through Jesus Christ our Lord," which is bound to make a portion of the company uncomfortable, and a perhaps even greater portion deeply uncomfortable on their behalf. Others give up the task of speaking to God more or less altogether, and turn the occasion into a speech to the gathered throng, framed by an address to God and a concluding Amen. The key is to achieve both reverence and attitude — a sense of depth but a willingness to name acute feelings and concerns. Many present, being perhaps familiar with the kinds of prayers mentioned earlier, may never have heard a prayer like this, which seeks to be gracious and merciful, gentle yet urgent.

OCCASIONS OF NATIONAL SIGNIFICANCE

Martin Luther King Jr. Day

Creator God, you set before us life and death. In the face of the Rev. Dr. Martin Luther King, Jr., you showed us what it means to choose life. Help us to choose life in every moment of every day. Help us to choose life in delighting in the wind, the rain, the stars, the sea, and the sun. Help us to choose life in enjoying the budding flower, the gurgling baby, the thrill of daybreak, and the still of the night. Help us to choose life in extending to one another the gentleness of touch, the openness of handshake, the comfort of embrace. Help us to choose life in speaking the truth rather than perpetuating lies, in facing our fears rather than running from them, in befriending strangers rather than protecting ourselves from them. Help us to choose life in walking the path of forgiveness rather than resentment, the road of reconciliation rather than bitterness, the way of healing rather than hatred. Help us to choose life in standing with those who suffer, weeping with those who weep, and rejoicing with those who rejoice. And help us to choose life even when it means facing our own mortality, so that, at the moment of our death, others may find in us your blessing. Amen.

Martin Luther King Jr. Day in mid-January has become a day when Americans reflect on the history of slavery and segregation, the contemporary state of racial politics in American society, and the still-unresolved issues on King's wider social agenda — remembering that he died supporting sanitation workers and perhaps was killed because of his opposition to the Vietnam War. Ceremonies on the day or on the Sunday prior to the day tend to be ones of non-sectarian piety, in which sharp edges are smoothed over, while substantial sections of the population stay away. This prayer is an attempt to find deeper truths while not avoiding the painful but brave legacy the day exists to commemorate.

Community Thanksgiving Service

Holy God, whose mercy is over all your works and whose will is ever directed to your children's good, make us people of compassion so that we may see one another through the same mercy you pour upon us. Help us to look to the good of one another. Draw near to those in need of an income and those facing unemployment, those who have lost meaningful work, and all seeking to find a job. Sustain and strengthen all who pray for food, all who hunger and thirst for the most basic things and worry about feeding their loved ones. Pour your grace upon families and men and women who need shelter, and those who need not only a home but a place to belong and to be loved as your child. Make your goodness known through the many ministries in this city that provide warm meals and a safe place to rest. Bless all whose lives are dedicated to the works of mercy and the volunteers who strengthen the Food Bank's mission.

Spirit of peace, give your blessing to families who gather. Bless the time together shared by parents who welcome children and grandchildren home. Bless all who anticipate the arrival of loved ones and prepare for thanksgiving feasts. Grace the gatherings and the meals, and the play and laughter within families and with friends so dear to us they are like family. Be with travelers on the highways, through airports, and on railroads. Stay close to all of us who are far from home and will be away from loved ones. Give your unfailing mercy to those who would make their way home but find the journey too painful and to any who simply can't go home again. Let your grace abound with your children who experience this time of year alone, without companions.

Lord God, whose abundance was found in a land flowing with milk and honey, shape us as people who trust your goodness will never run dry. Like the taste of milk and honey on our lips, make our lives abound in the sweetness of your promise that you have given us a place to belong and an everlasting home. Be a sure companion to immigrants who have left one country for an unknown one, left family members behind, and taken risky journeys. Walk beside us when we travel unfamiliar paths in life and when we wander without a clear path to follow. In uncharted places, meet us anew in your love.

Gather to your heart our prayers, O God, that in these days of cele-bration, our thanksgiving may come not only from our lips but from our very lives as we praise you for such lovingkindness lavished upon us. Amen.

A community-wide service around the Thanksgiving holiday requires a prayer that reaches people of varied faith backgrounds. This prayer was written specifically for worship shared between Christians and Jews. It addresses shared community concerns and incorporates the organization receiving the offering. The prayer embraces the language of Hebrew scripture to provide image and metaphor ("land flowing with milk and honey," "whose mercy is over all your works") and also to find language to address God. "Lord God" is a name that would be heard differently by Jews and Christians, but is a shared name for God. The prayer also delves into a present-day theme which grows out of the story of the first Thanksgiving: the story of immigrants in a new land. This prayer does not address the topic of Native Americans but very well could; however, that might better belong in a confessional prayer on such an occasion. The danger in praying at a time where the holiday is a national observation which isn't part of the liturgical calendar is that the intercessor might be tempted to use language of public discourse rather than language of scripture. This prayer interprets the Thanksgiving holiday through the story of faith.

Anniversary of September 11

Holy God, look with mercy on the lives shattered by the attacks of 9/11.

Be in the imagination of anyone who works or lives in a tall building, and wonders, or who regularly boards or works on an airplane, and dreads, or who resides in New York City or Washington, DC, and can't forget, or who sees the face of a stranger, and fears.

Be among all who mourn, and will continue to mourn; who feel hatred and fury, and search for targets and culprits; who seek to offer security, at airports, in espionage, on the battlefield, or in diplomacy.

Bless Muslims, who feel shame at what was done in their name; bless all who work for a new relationship between Christianity, Judaism, and Islam, and between America and the Arab world; and empower all who seek to make beauty out of ashes and find you in the dust.

Look with favor upon those whose lives lie in the dust of 9/11. Let eternal light shine upon them, as with your saints in eternity. Grant them eternal rest, O Lord, because you are merciful. Amen.

One of the most significant things to do on the anniversary of 9/11 is to ensure a Muslim voice is prominent in the proceedings. Here there's a conscious effort to echo some forms of Muslim expression — for example the emphasis on God as merciful. There's also a deliberate policy of not regarding the attacks as attacks on the United States, or of assuming all those who died were Americans. The prayer was offered at a performance of Mozart's Requiem and some of the words echo the words of the text.

OCCASIONS FOR A VIGIL

A Vigil against Violence

(1)

God of mercy, you see us in our neediness, our nakedness, and our nervousness. We tremble before you in the face of death, and we lament before you in the wake of the waste, and the loss, and the crime, and the horror, and the injustice of these terrible deaths.

Take our anger at this violence and turn it into something beautiful to enrich your kingdom. Take our bewilderment and frustration at the difficulty in identifying culprits and gaining convictions and turn them into energy for making peaceful communities and creating alternatives to hatred.

Be close to us in our powerlessness. Give us friends who can sit with us in times of wordless misery. Bless us with strength to face each new morning, even when we fear it may bring further grief and sorrow. Walk with us when we feel guilty at being the ones who were spared, when others were taken.

Most of all, redeem these broken, bleeding, and buried lives. Redeem them eternally in the company of heaven. Redeem them in the healing of wounds and the drying of tears and the deepening of friendships. And redeem them in the work of those who seek a life beyond violence, a future beyond hatred, and a truth beyond bitterness. Show us your broken heart through this veil of ours. Amen.

(2)

God of consolation, we bring you our aching hearts: open your heart to us;

we bring you our questioning minds: show us your thoughts and your ways;

we bring you our anger and despair: show us your compassion and patience;

we bring you our fear: show us your steadfastness;

we bring you our aloneness: show us your companionship;

we bring you our weariness: show us your new life;

we bring you our failure: show us your forgiveness;

we bring you our grief: show us your embrace;

we bring you our emptiness: show us your abundance;

we bring you our tears: show us your face;

we bring you our fragility: show us your tenderness;

we bring you our hunger: feed us now and evermore.

Give us the courage to face the new day, hope to live in your time, and the wisdom to look to you for what only you can do. Amen.

The settings in which these prayers were offered were explicitly multi-faith, although in a way that suppresses difference rather than one that relishes diversity. And appropriately so, because the focus was not on range of belief but on solidarity of commitment in the face of multiple violent deaths in the community. There are always plenty of voices seeking legislative change and the intervention of authorities; these prayers recognize that epic context, but seek to engage the lyric reality of grief, anger, bewilderment, and fear. One thing that always causes tension on such occasions is over-hasty calls for forgiveness. These prayers don't make such a move, preferring to explore the complexity of the process of reconciliation, rather than prescribe a specific outcome.

Vigil after a Massacre

God of justice, the blood of your children cries to you from the ground. . . . God of mercy, look upon those whose lives have been seared by a violence they will never erase from their mind's eye. . . . God of tenderness, be close to those whose hearts are broken. . . . God of wisdom, speak through the mouths of those who lead the university and town, those who will conduct funerals and counsel the mourners. . . . God of grace, burn in the hearts of those who have to face public scrutiny, the security forces, the administrators, the decision makers, as everyone searches for someone to blame. . . . God of hope, be with everyone at [X] as they begin to imagine how they can be a community again. . . . Be with all parents and relatives and children. . . . And with those wondering how to trust in another day. . . . God of our imaginations, transform our thoughts from fear to compassion. . . . And make us people who learn to love as you love, even when it breaks our hearts. . . . Amen.

A massacre is an event for which a whole community will put down everything and gather at very short notice. It's vital to be prepared to pray in such a way that affirms the unity of feeling, however gruesome the reality may be. This prayer was offered before several hundred people at an interfaith vigil within 24 hours of a notorious massacre. So soon after the event is too early to refer in any significant way to the perpetrator — the details are not fully known; more important is to reach the lyric depth of the pain and shock, and to frame the event with the wider goods which have been so disturbed, but will become the source of regeneration in due time. The ellipses indicate that periods of silence were kept after each sentence: the role of intercession at a vigil is largely to structure silence.

OCCASIONS OF INTERNATIONAL CRISIS

Prayer at the Outbreak of Conflict

God of justice and mercy, we come before you tonight in grief and fear regarding the reports we have heard from a very troubled land. Look with mercy on the broken relationships and damaged trust that lie behind the current violence.

Be close to the parties at the center of the conflict, and the politicians and people of influence they represent. Transform the tribal allegiances now set against one another. Strengthen those who seek to end corruption and those striving to restore confidence in the political process.

Be with all who mourn, bind up any who are wounded, restore those whose lives have been mentally, physically, and emotionally scarred, and be close to everyone who lives each hour in fear.

Deepen ties between this community and the people of that troubled land. Show us how their struggle is our struggle, and inscribe in our lives the ways we can be present to them in their hour of need.

> *Come among us now with wisdom and understanding, counsel and inward strength, that we may learn how to respond, know how to react, discern whom to trust, and discover what to hope for. Help us find strength in one another and faith in your love. Amen.*

When widespread violence breaks out, a bland prayer for peace won't do. Neither is it particularly helpful to show off one's extraordinarily extensive knowledge of foreign affairs. The important points are to recognize dismay, to acknowledge people who may have personal connections to a troubled place, to offer humility and a desire for understanding, and to name the powerlessness of not knowing what to think, to hope, or to say.

A Prayer for Haiti

> *God of the living and the dead, we wail in grief at the pain and loss and horror and distress of our brothers and sisters in Haiti. We do not understand your ways — that those who already suffer the most, now suffer so much more. Lead us to repentance, that we who have sinned so much are punished so little, and they who already struggle have now impossible burdens to bear. Where people are still breathing under collapsed buildings, give them air and hope and courageous searchers. Where children are injured or orphaned, find them trusted friends and generous caregivers. Where despair is infectious and disease or looting spreads, bring patience and forbearance and healing and strength to conquer temptation. And when others look with compassion from afar, release resources, empower expertise, shape political will, and bring deliverance for your people in their distress. Through him who was crushed and bruised for us, in the comfort of your Holy Spirit. Amen.*

One ministry that is possible in the internet age is for a priest or pastor to issue a prayer within hours of an international disaster. When people feel powerless and don't know how to respond, or when people gather in public places and don't know how to articulate appropriate words, a prayer like this can not only give them something to hold on to, but tangibly shape the way the conversation takes place. This prayer was issued shortly after the devastating Haiti earthquake of January 2010. It seeks to engage horror, grief, guilt, and questions about the justice of God. Because it is a written prayer, it's possible to include a Trinitarian conclusion — which can simply be removed if deemed inappropriate.

A Prayer for Syria

God of mercy and grace, look with compassion on your people who face the horror of civil war.

As in your Son you were a refugee, walk with those who flee terror and abandon home and livelihood and loved ones.

As you anticipated a day when a house would be divided against itself, be with all who find that neighbors, relatives, colleagues, and friends have become enemies, spies, and soldiers.

As you breathe through your church, move in the hearts of Christians as they seek to uphold their faith, their integrity, their longing for justice, their spirit of forgiveness.

As you judge the nations, give wisdom and restraint to all who feel the urgency of doing something visible and instant, however destructive and violent that something might be.

As once you first led your Son's followers in this land to be called Christians, make this bleeding nation again one where your glory is revealed as helpless baby, crucified redeemer, and risen Lord, that as today so many know the agony of your cross, each may come to share the Sabbath of your resurrection. Amen.

When TV screens are filled with images of horror and destruction, and it's not clear what Western governments can do about an international crisis without making it worse, the best single thing a pastor can do is to create ways for people to intercede — tangibly, in a vigil, or more simply, by composing a prayer that can be circulated or placed on a website and then used on the following Sunday in a worship service. This prayer seeks to bring the conflict in Syria close to home by exploring the war from personal, church, and political perspectives, before ending with a plea for resurrection to emerge out of crucifixion. The reference to the "first Christians" from Acts 11:26 is technically incorrect, because Antioch is just across the border in Turkey: but the point is to remember that Syria is not simply a faraway Muslim land but a country with profound Christian history and significant Christian presence.

OCCASIONS OF UNIVERSITY LIFE

Prayer for Those Beginning Undergraduate Life

Lord God, you show us your face in the form of beauty, truth, and goodness. Through the beauty of this place and the intricate wonders of our courses of study, help us live lives that enrich the lives of others and cherish beauty in unheralded people and places in your world. Through research and discovery, wrestling with ideas and listening to strangers, take us deeper into truth and make us a people without fear of the different or the unknown. And through forging and sustaining friendships, sharing and receiving wisdom, and making commitments of grace in the face of one another's need, form us in the habits of goodness, that others may see your face in ours. Amen.

The convocation of new undergraduates is an event for the entire university community, in which all present ought to feel welcome and included. The challenge for the one leading prayers is to offer the intensity and focus of a Christian prayer without using the same vocabulary, in such a way that all

143

can endorse, but within which Christians can still recognize themselves. This prayer adopts as its structure the Platonic forms of beauty, truth, and goodness and inscribes them with content that has resonance for Christians and non-Christians alike.

Baccalaureate

God of grace and glory, we thank you for the gift of this university: for the wisdom we have gained, the adventures we have had, and the friends we have made. Make us mindful of those who have made our education possible, any who for sad reasons are not here today, and all who lack the opportunities we enjoy. Heal and transform all that has taken place here that we mourn and regret. Open our eyes to what we have yet to learn about ourselves, humanity, and the world. Help us to treat each new place to which we may move as a new seat of learning; each new friend and colleague as new faculty; and each new challenge and trial as a new curriculum. And fill us with your goodness, your truth, and your beauty, that all whom we meet may find in us a blessing. Amen.

Commencement

God of mercy and grace, we thank you for the precious gift of our college years. Take the knowledge and experience we have gained, and turn them into wisdom. Take our discoveries and adventures and transform them into a lifetime spent living truth, pursuing justice, searching for peace, seeking you. Take our regrets, our mistakes, our hurts, and our false starts, and heal them into gentler compassion, greater understanding, and truer concern for those who can only dream of experiencing a day like today. Take our pride and sense of achievement and color them with humble gratitude for family, teachers, and mentors who have taught us, trained us, and helped us

> *on our way. Take our fears and shape them into wonder at the world you have made, and joy at the companions you have given us within it. Take our hearts, our hands, our souls, and our voices, and make them a melody of rejoicing, a sunrise of wonder, and a symphony of beauty, today and every day. Amen.*

The "graduation exercises" of a university may include both a baccalaureate ceremony, with sermon, prayers, anthems, hymns, and a presidential address, and the commencement, with the conferral of degrees and a distinguished and student speaker. The mood at the former is stately: the prayer seeks to affirm a sense of lifelong learning, as students leave to a sometimes uncertain future, but one that may be redeemed by seeing it as a continuation of a process engaged by habits learned at the university. The latter occasion is one of uninhibited celebration: so there is no point trying to be too solemn; but it's still the only place in the ceremony where it's possible to refer to anything negative in the college experience, so this opportunity is pursued in a tone of redemption.

OCCASIONS OF PUBLIC GATHERING

A Prayer for a Blood Donor Campaign by the Red Cross

God of creation, of healing, and of everlasting life, you give us the gift of blood to course through our veins and bring nutrition, oxygen, and restoration to our limbs and organs. Through this meal in your company you restore our bodies, invigorate our minds, and nourish our souls. Through this fellowship of grace and bond of service, make us veins and arteries for your world, that we may be messengers of your peace, couriers of your justice, and vehicles of your love; that your world may know through our ministry that all things come from you, because you are our heart. Amen.

Part of being a priest or pastor is being ready to be called upon to pray for or bless a myriad range of people, objects, places, and events. This is a prayer requested by a gathering of those who organize blood donations. Rather than be content with generic benedictions, this prayer seeks to identify blood as the heart of faith and a metaphor for new life — albeit in a way that doesn't specifically mention the blood of Christ at the Last Supper, on the cross, and at the Eucharistic table. Ministry in many cases means taking people a little more seriously than they take themselves.

A Prayer at the Opening of a New Social Housing Development

God of transformation, you have made a dwelling place among us, and made yourself known in houses of brick and stone as well as in open spaces with trees and grass. We praise you for the gift of [X]. We thank you for the partnerships between local residents and public, private, and non-profit agencies that have brought it about. We recall that where people gather in goodwill to seek the welfare of your city, you are in the midst of them. Be in the midst of this neighborhood and this community today. Give its new residents a spirit of wisdom and understanding, a spirit of counsel and inward strength, a spirit of generosity and hospitality, that others may find a blessing in their company, gain inspiration to embark on such transformation themselves, and leave with a renewed sense of what you can do and what they can do; only to return with new ideas, new partnerships, new faith, new self-respect, and a new appreciation for what it means to build, and what it means to plant. Lord God, you have built and planted in us. May what you have built here and in us never decay, and what you have planted here and in us ever grow. Amen.

After several years seeking to be an agent of reconciliation in a community, a priest or pastor may be invited to play a significant role as a mediator in a dispute or as a speaker of joy at a time of celebration. In this case a patch of land that had been the subject of disharmony was turned into social housing and a park that brought pleasure and pride to a wide range of local organizations, businesses, and authorities. Here the prayer weaves in the language of Isaiah and the hope of rebuilding Jerusalem with a reflection on what is built (the housing) and what is planted (the park) and the tangible and metaphorical difference between the two.

A Prayer for an Interfaith Coalition of Volunteers in Public Schools

[You're going to want to keep your eyes open for this prayer. Hold your two hands open with palms up in front of you.]

Holy God, we look at our hands and give thanks for those who taught us to write and to read, to hold books and pencils. In a moment of silence, we remember those who taught us to have hands of gentleness and peacemaking and those who have shown us how to have hands of compassion and committed devotion. . . . Make our thankful hearts abound in ways that bring you joy.

[Now look at the hands of the neighbor on your right or left.]

Holy God, we look at one another's hands and give thanks for what we share. We celebrate the stories that have brought our neighbors here today though their stories may be different from our own. In a moment of silence, we anticipate the many lives that will be touched by our neighbor's hands and celebrate one another's willingness to reach into the lives of children. . . . Take our eager hearts and show us how to rejoice in one another.

[Now look back at your hands.]

Holy God, we look back at our own hands and we see the hands of children in schools throughout [city]. In a moment of silence, we give thanks for the lives of the children whose faces we know best. . . . Help us as a community to nurture these youngest hands, that they may become people of patience and perseverance in the face of personal

challenges, people of creativity and courage in the midst of poverty,
people of peacemaking and gentleness in a world of war, that their
touch may become a gift to [city].

At the start of a new year, make our open hands a sign of the hope
you've placed in our hearts and make us ready to receive the many
gifts you have to give us in one another and in the children of this city.
Amen.

Prayer in public schools is a thorny subject, and yet volunteer groups who seek to strengthen low-income public schools may be motivated and sustained by faith and seek out the blessing of clergy upon their involvement. This is a prayer that depends upon the intercessor's attention and pacing to allow those gathered to populate the intercessions with faces and stories from their own experience. It is an example of providing a structure in a public setting where expectations for prayer may range widely; this particular setting was Jewish, Muslim, and Christian. And it is structured in a way to allow listeners to call to mind specific people and dwell upon those individuals with care.

A Prayer at a Pilgrimage for Justice and Peace

God of hope, you give us the tradition of pilgrimage; in the 84th Psalm
you tell us "how blest are they, who going through the vale of misery,
use it for a well; and the pools are filled with water." Look upon all
who today are going through the vale of misery; we keep a moment of
silent lament in solidarity with them now. . . . Be close to those gath-
ered to walk through the vale of misery today, that they may use it
for a well. Bless their tears, that their tears may nourish one another
and those who hunger and thirst for righteousness. Encourage their
pilgrimage, that as they walk they may come to a deeper understand-
ing both of the nature of their goal and the reality that you walk with
them. Be their partner on the road, the pillar of cloud ahead, and
their shining star above.

God of mercy, take from our hearts the matters with which we struggle and from our backs the burdens that weigh us down today. Infuse our lives with peace — in this country among people of different nationalities and races and religions and classes, and in this town between many who look at one another with fear and enmity. Bring peace between humanity and the earth; shape the hearts and budgets of business leader and legislator and consumer and traveler to live more simply and more in tune with your creation. Inaugurate peace between this country and other nations and within nations whose conflicts are underwritten by finance and arms from this land. God of healing and transformation, strengthen those initiatives where your presence and wisdom is bearing fruit; work within practices of fair trade, in the hearts of all seeking to legislate just wages and working conditions and ensure such legislation is honored, among any striving to uphold families and places where people find nurture, stability, encouragement, and love, and those incorporating immigrants into the local economy, culture, language, and pride. Help us to see ourselves as you see us, to love as you love, to hurt when you hurt, and to walk where you walk. And let justice flow like a never-failing stream. Amen.

The ecumenical — or interfaith — gathering for justice and peace is a moment where prayer can quickly descend into lecture, devotional meditation can be overrun by clichés of solidarity, and faith can be rapidly instrumentalized for a cause that's as vague as it's widely held. The important thing in a prayer of this kind, particularly if one cannot speak in Trinitarian language, is to name the issues closest to people's hearts, but to do so in a way that sounds like a petition and not a manifesto. The secret here is to begin with a recognition that brokenness lies within us, not just among the "needy" whom the "powerful" culpably neglect.

Wedding

(1)

Eternal God, whose love rejoices with us in times of celebration, lavish your grace upon X and Y in the promises they make today. Through this day of celebration, draw us closer to one another and to your extravagant love for us, both now and forever. Bless the families of X and Y. Pour your grace upon the many ways the lives of these families will meet and touch and be shared. Give them abiding peace in times of change and expectant hope in times of discovery. Bless their loved ones who celebrate with them as saints in glory, [names], whose love abides still. Through the relentless joy of your Holy Spirit, make the wedding feast shared here be for all of us an anticipation of your heavenly banquet, when heaven and earth shall be one.

✳︎ ✳︎ ✳︎

God, whose Son showed us the most perfect way to love one another, give X and Y wisdom and devotion in the ordering of their common life, that each may be to the other a counselor in perplexity, a comfort in sorrow, and a companion in celebration. Give them grace, when they hurt each other, to recognize and acknowledge each their own fault, and to seek one another's forgiveness and yours. And give them such tenderness in their shared affection for one another that they may reach out in love and concern to others. Through the making of promises here today, show your grace to all married couples in the places where they most need it and help them grow in mutuality as companions with one another and with you.

✳︎ ✳︎ ✳︎

God, whose love is made perfect in us through the power of the Holy Spirit, bless and sanctify X and Y with your Holy Spirit as they come now to join in marriage. Grant that they may give their vows to one another in the strength of your steadfast love, and enable them to

grow in love and peace with you and one another all their days. Bless
them, Lord God, so that their life together will give glory to you above.
All these prayers we ask in the name of Jesus Christ, who with the
Father and the Spirit we praise forever. Amen.

Making the most of the prayers at a wedding can deepen the occasion from being an event to being worship. While much of a wedding consists of the pastor speaking to the people for God and enabling the couple to speak to one another in the vows, the time of prayer represents a marked shift where the pastor speaks to God. This prayer seeks to incorporate language from traditional United Methodist and Episcopal liturgies while infusing it with an opening petition that captures the mood of the day and, at the same time, gathers up pastoral concerns.

———

(2)

Lord God our Father, you have given us the gift of marriage; make X
and Y be for one another a magnifying glass through which each sees
the world more truthfully, a mirror in which each sees themselves
more honestly, and a tender embrace through which each loves the
world more compassionately. As you are making X and Y a blessing
to one another, make their marriage a blessing to others, that in their
home, family, friends, and strangers may find generosity and under-
standing. In their work, may colleagues and clients find challenge
and reward, and in their play may others see the dance of your Spirit.

* * *

Almighty God, in Christ you show us you reign not only over life but
over death; give us hope in the face of fear, trust in the face of despair,
joy in the face of dread. You have empowered Z to be among us now.
Give him everything he needs to live these days with beauty, dignity,
and joy. Give us grace to live each hour as if it were our last, that at
the close of day we may look to you, and to one another, and be able
to offer its thoughts and words and deeds as a sacrament of praise,
and a reflection of your glory.

* * *

*Loving God, you bless and challenge us with the gift of one another;
send your Spirit on the new community inaugurated by this marriage; comfort those who up to this day felt they had first call on X's
and Y's hearts, as they find a new way of relating to the two of them
now as one body. Hold in your heart all who are not with us today,
among them those friends and family that are rejoicing with us, and
any separated from us by death or estrangement*

* * *

*Take this love of X and Y, and make it something beyond their imag-
ining, that through it they and others may witness and enjoy the wondrous love that is in your heart, which will finally flood your creation
with joy; through Jesus Christ our Lord. Amen.*

The most straightforward context for leading intercession is where all those
present are known and trusted by one another; where the need is explicit and
understood by all, and where what's required is an intercessor who is able to
weave the longings of the congregation into the story of God in such a way
that all present can sense God's hand in the outcome of their prayers. That
doesn't often happen, but sometimes it does, and here, in a chapter largely
given to improvisation in unusual contexts, is an example in what might be
called an "ideal" — if very sad — circumstance.

A man whose daughter was to be married learned he had only a few days
to live. His daughter hastily brought forward her marriage plans by several
months, and nine people gathered sharing the couple's joy but knowing it
would be the last time they would all be together. The daughter walked up
a very long aisle all on her own, hoping her father could take her arm for the
last five yards; but in the end even that was too much. He died five days later.
These were the intercessions offered on the wedding day.

Funeral

(1)

*God of intimate creativity, you weave our lives in secret and shape our
lives through mysterious wonders; we thank you for the gift of X. We
praise you for the careers he formed and the lives he saved. We rejoice
in the detail of his surgeon's art and professor's craft. Uphold all who
stood alongside him, and empower everyone who gives and receives
care in Y Hospital today. Give wisdom and skill to its department of
surgery, its chair, and all who carry forward its mission. Inspire each
one of us to bring healing and truth into the lives of others.*

✳ ✳ ✳

*God of the future and the past, you at the same time ask everything
of us and give us everything we need to follow you. Help us, as we
grieve X's loss, to see your life in his. Look upon the tiniest details of
our lives; show us when those details are invitations to encounter
you. Give us the humility not always to assume it is for us to enter
the Promised Land, but instead to find our role in making it possible
for others to do so. Bless those who will feel X's loss every day of their
lives, Z and all her family; when they are bewildered at the loss they
have sustained, when they long for words of comfort, yet find them
hard to hear, turn their grief to truer living, their affliction to firmer
hope and their sadness to deeper joy.*

✳ ✳ ✳

*God of innocent joy, you love each one of us yet love each of us as if
we were the only one. Give us grace to use aright the time that you
have left for us on earth, that we might so enjoy the glories of your
creation that we become witnesses of hope, facing our own mortality
with patience and courage.*

✳ ✳ ✳

*Bring X, O Lord God, at his last awakening into the house and gate
of heaven, to enter into that gate and dwell in that house, where*

there shall be no darkness nor dazzling, but one equal light; no noise nor silence, but one equal music; no fears nor hopes, but one equal possession; no ends nor beginnings, but one equal eternity; in the habitations of thy glory and dominion, world without end. Amen.

These prayers were offered at the funeral of a surgeon who died at an advanced age after a long illness. They include thankfulness, proceed to lyric and epic reflection on his life, and increasingly incorporate the language of traditional prayers, until in the end they become folded into a centuries-old prayer that in its speaking incorporates the dead person into the communion of saints. The effort throughout is to mix dignity, intimacy, and traditional faith.

———

(2)

Everlasting God, you created life and death; we thank you for the gift of X. We thank you for his joy, his wit, his style, his power with words, his friendship, his love of basketball, of his family, of fashion, of fun. We thank you for what you showed us of yourself in him — your abundant life, your companionship with us, your shimmers of joy, your never-ending love.

Father God, you know the agony of a son's death. Be close to us as we express our anger, fear, and sadness. Embrace X's close family and friends in their horror and dismay. You know our hearts and share our sorrows. When we long for words of comfort, yet find them hard to hear, turn our grief to truer living, our affliction to firmer hope, and our sadness to deeper joy.

Broken Jesus, your pain is shared today by those who grieve. Bless this community: students, faculty, staff, alums, and all who look to this place for work and play and study and discovery. Remember us, as you remember X; bind up our wounds, bring us face to face with one another in compassion and shared humanity, and sustain us in continuing to treasure all that X held dear.

Transforming Spirit, bring X at his last awakening into the house and gate of heaven, to enter into that gate and dwell in that house, where there shall be no darkness nor dazzling, but one equal light; no noise nor silence, but one equal music; no fears nor hopes, but one equal possession; no ends nor beginnings, but one equal eternity; in the habitations of thy glory and dominion, world without end. Amen.

These prayers were said at the funeral of a student who died alone in a tragic accident. They end with the same conclusion as the previous example, and they begin with a similar note of thanksgiving; but in between the tone is rather different. The service began with a tone of aching lament: here the mood is to name specific things to mourn and treasure. Again there is a blend of traditional language and vivid references to the young person and the manner of death. The term "us" is unproblematic because it clearly means everyone gathered for the ceremony.

CHECKLIST FOR PREPARING
THE PRAYERS OF THE PEOPLE

Gather images, phrases, and ideas from:

☐ Church year, liturgical season

☐ Scripture for the day

☐ Worship/sermon themes

☐ Lyrics of hymns or other music

Identify concerns:

☐ Global/national events of significance

☐ The church universal

☐ Issues of the local community

☐ The sick

☐ The recently departed

☐ Congregational cares and other particular needs

Then you are ready to write your prayers.

After writing the prayers, review what you have.

☐ Check to be sure your terms for addressing God express the multiple
dimensions of who God is.

☐ Look for a balance of address to God in the breadth of Trinitarian language.

☐ Look for vigorous imperative verbs throughout, except in places where the "being" verbs ("be present to . . . ," "be with all who . . .") are best.

☐ Check on any place you've used the third person. Remember God should never be referred to in the third person. Check to be sure you're always speaking to God about people's needs, not speaking to people directly.

☐ Review any use of "all who" or "those who" or "any who" to ensure you're not speaking of a "they" which should really be an "us." Check to be sure you haven't used a phrase like "those who" too often.

☐ Check on any place you've used "we" to be sure it is truly all-inclusive. Be careful about the use of "we" and keep it to a minimum. Be sure you've avoided social commentary and phrases that pass implicit judgments.

☐ Look for a balance of "lyric" congregational cares and "epic" concerns beyond the local church.

☐ Make certain that, at the beginning, there is a clear invitation to prayer.

☐ Ensure that the ending is suitable, satisfying, and not abrupt.

☐ Check to be sure the expectations for congregational responses are clear, either in print or by verbal instruction, and that any response is succinct and doesn't require use of a reminder on page or screen, so worshipers can remain focused throughout.